Read Write Inc.
PHONICS

Phonics Handbook

Series developed by Ruth Miskin

OXFORD
UNIVERSITY PRESS

OXFORD
UNIVERSITY PRESS

Great Clarendon Street, Oxford OX2 6DP

Oxford University Press is a department of the University of Oxford.
It furthers the University's objective of excellence in research, scholarship,
and education by publishing worldwide in

Oxford New York

Auckland Cape Town Dar es Salaam Hong Kong Karachi
Kuala Lumpur Madrid Melbourne Mexico City Nairobi
New Delhi Shanghai Taipei Toronto

With offices in

Argentina Austria Brazil Chile Czech Republic France Greece
Guatemala Hungary Italy Japan Poland Portugal Singapore
South Korea Switzerland Thailand Turkey Ukraine Vietnam

Oxford is a registered trade mark of Oxford University Press
in the UK and in certain other countries

First published as *The Storybook and Get Writing! Handbook* by Ruth Miskin Literacy Ltd 2005

First published as the *Read Write Inc. Phonics Handbook* by Oxford University Press 2006

This edition published by Oxford University Press 2009

British Library Cataloguing in Publication Data

Data available

ISBN 978-0-19-846938-4

3 5 7 9 10 8 6 4 2

Printed in Great Britain by Ashford Colour Press, Gosport, Hants

Paper used in the production of this book is a natural, recyclable product
made from wood grown in sustainable forests. The manufacturing process
conforms to the environmental regulations of the country of origin.

Contents

Introduction

Dear Teacher,

While I was a headteacher in London I began to devise a programme that would get all children learning to read and write quickly and easily. The programme, *Read Write Inc. Phonics*, has now been widely used and tested and is hugely successful in many schools.

At the core of *Read Write Inc. Phonics* is the lively and vigorous teaching of synthetic phonics. Children learn the 44 common sounds in the English language and how to sound-blend words for reading (decoding) at the same time as developing handwriting skills and spelling (encoding). Crucially, they read lively Storybooks and Non-fiction books with words they can decode, so they achieve early success in reading. The more sounds they know the greater the range of texts they can read.

As children are taught to decode and encode, they are also taught to comprehend and to compose – out loud. The quicker their decoding the more they comprehend; and, the quicker their encoding the more they write of what they have composed out loud.

As children have early success in reading, teachers in Year 2 (Primary 3) and above can put all their energy into encouraging children to read widely and often: comics and computer games, as well as literature that will propel their vocabulary growth. Their children can use words in their writing like diminutive, impenetrable, surreptitious - because they've talked about them in the books they read.

And, most importantly, because they read as easily as breathing, they begin to develop a way of thinking necessary for all school learning – discursive thought; the ability to hold and develop a complex network of ideas and arguments.

Teachers, and teaching assistants, really enjoy teaching *Read Write Inc. Phonics*. Firstly, because there is nothing more rewarding than seeing children learn to read and write so quickly and secondly, because the high level of planning gives new teachers practical day-to-day guidance and experienced teachers the energy and time to plan creatively.

Ruth Miskin

What is Read Write Inc.?

There are four programmes:

Read Write Inc. Phonics is an inclusive literacy programme for all children learning to read in Foundation to Year 4 (P1 to P5) currently reading at National Curriculum level 2b (Level B/First Level - Scotland; Level 2 - Northern Ireland; Level 2 - Wales) or below. It is also suitable for children in older year groups who have significant learning difficulties, including specific literacy problems. Children will achieve a level 2a (Level B/First Level - Scotland; Level 2 - Northern Ireland; Level 2 - Wales) and above when they have completed the programme.

Read Write Inc. Comprehension follows on from *Read Write Inc. Phonics* and is a series of weekly modules for children in Years 2–4 (P3 to P5) who can decode (read) very well. The programme aims to take children to National Curriculum level 3 (Level C/Second Level - Scotland; Level 3 - Northern Ireland; Level 3 - Wales). There are 15 fiction texts and 15 non-fiction texts, each with a set of core comprehension and composition activities.

Read Write Inc. Fresh Start follows a similar format to *Read Write Inc. Phonics* but is aimed at children in Years 5, 6 and 7 (P6, P7 and S1/P8) who are currently reading below National Curriculum level 3 (Level C/Second Level - Scotland; Level 3 - Northern Ireland; Level 3 - Wales). It uses age-appropriate texts and is also suitable for older students who have been invited to take part.

Read Write Inc. Spelling is a quick 10-minutes-a-day spelling programme for children who can read at National Curriculum level 2a (Level B/First Level - Scotland; Level 2 - Northern Ireland; Level 2 - Wales) and above. There are three Get Spelling! books and a Spelling Log Book. The programme takes children from level 2a to level 5. (Level B/First Level - Scotland; Level 2 - Northern Ireland; Level 2 - Wales to Level D/E/Second Level - Scotland; Level 5 - Northern Ireland; Level 5 - Wales). It is suitable for any age.

The *Read Write Inc.* programmes teach reading and writing. Talking is a critical and integral element of the programme. There is no bolt-on 'speaking and listening' module.

Read Write Inc. Phonics resources

Learning the letters and sounds

Speed Sounds Cards Sets 1, 2 and 3

Introduce all 44 sounds and corresponding graphemes, with lively mnemonics.

Picture-Sounds Cards

118 cards for use in Speed Sounds lessons.

Learning blending and segmenting

Magnetic Sounds Cards

Help children identify letter shapes and develop skills of blending and segmenting.

Applying phonic knowledge to reading books

Ditty Photocopy Masters and Ditty Books

Short decodable passages to give children practice in sound blending: an important bridge between reading single words and reading stories.

Storybooks

75 decodable Storybooks levelled to children's phonic knowledge.

15 Set A Storybooks for further practice.

Teacher support for Read Write Inc. Phonics

Phonics Handbook

Full guidance on implementing *Read Write Inc. Phonics* including:

- initial and on-going assessment
- *Storybooks* and *Get Writing!* Books
- timetables
- practical help on partner work
- classroom management.

Speed Sounds Lesson Plans

Essential lesson plans for how to teach each Speed Sound.

Softwar

Speed Sounds Set 1, 2, and 3 CD-ROM

Sounds Picture frieze

Colour wall display of the 44 sounds and mnemonics.

Speed Sounds posters

Simple and Complex Sounds Posters for quick reviews of letter-sound correspondences.

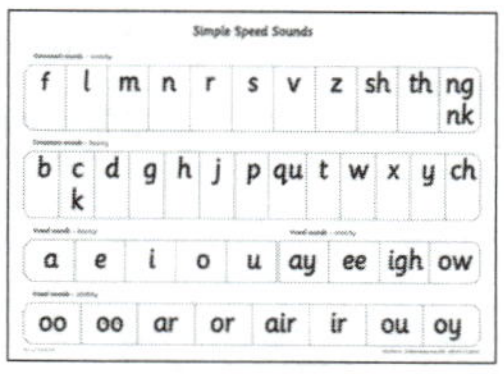

Green and Red Words Cards

Green Word Cards for children to practise word blending for reading.

Red Word Cards for children to practise reading words with tricky spellings.

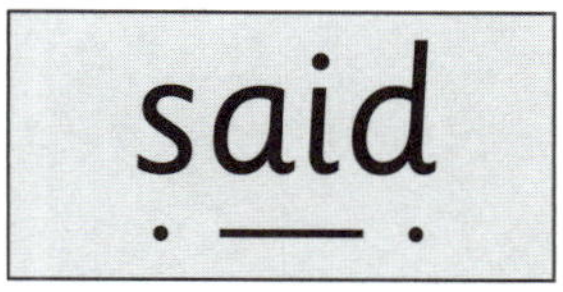

Non-fiction

35 non-fiction titles for further phonic practice, at home and at school.

Get Writing! Books

Seven *Get Writing!* books for children to embed their phonic knowledge, spelling, punctuation and compose texts.

Interactive Stories

14 of the Storybooks on CD-ROM, with accompanying activities.

Phonemes Pronunciation Guide DVD

Shows how to pronounce the 44 phonemes as 'pure' sounds for effective blending and segmenting.

The simple view of reading

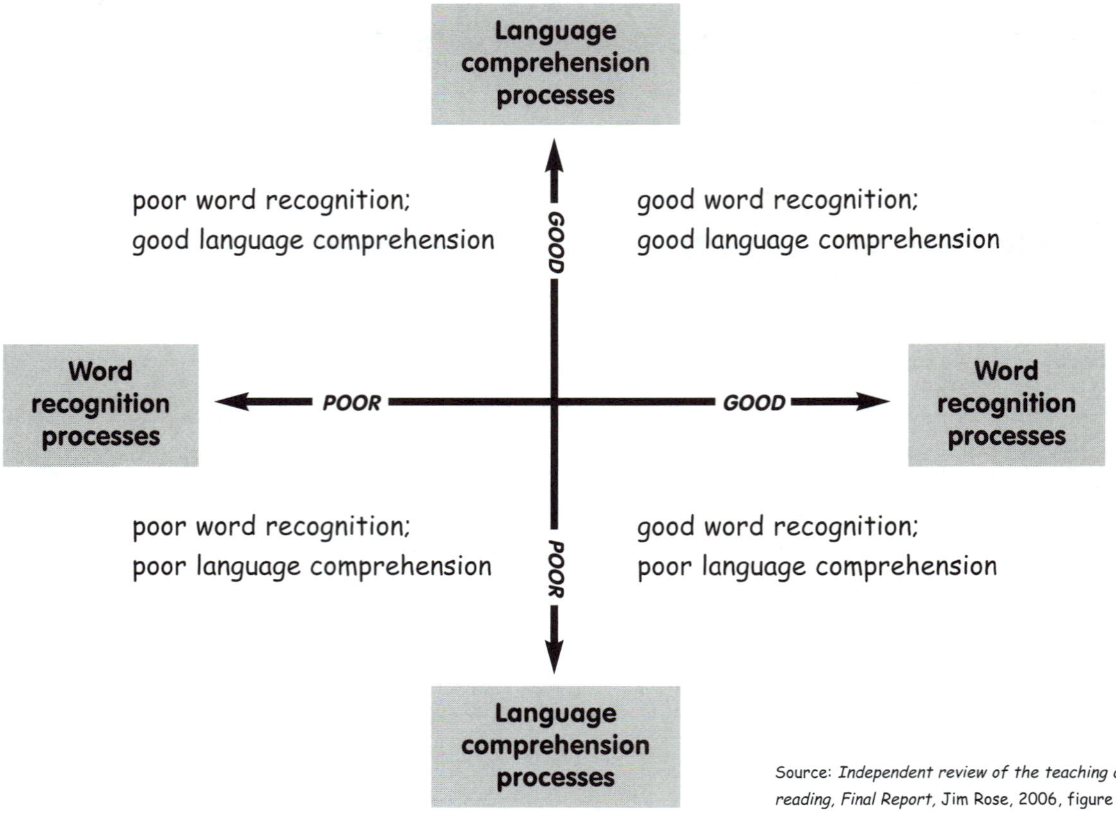

Source: *Independent review of the teaching of early reading, Final Report,* Jim Rose, 2006, figure 1, page 40.

The government now recognises the model of the 'simple view of reading', recommended in the Rose Report (2006). Children need to have both good word recognition and good oral language comprehension in order to read.

Good word recognition is dependent upon decoding rapidly. Good oral language comprehension is dependent upon the deliberate use of talk.

As readers we need to decode rapidly before we can take in even the most simple message. To understand complex passages we need to decode as easily as breathing so all our energy can go into comprehending the message on the page. Without speedy decoding comprehension is impossible.

Language comprehension begins at birth and develops throughout life. Learning to read well takes 18 months to two years. However, when children begin reading well, their language comprehension accelerates hugely. The Rose Report makes the distinction between two phases in a child's academic life: 'Learn to read' and 'Read to learn.'

Good oral language comprehension and the deliberate use of talk is vital in both phases.

The 'Learn to read' phase is time-limited; children should be out of this phase by the age of seven. The books they read in this phase contain fewer words than are in their oral language comprehension.

The 'Read to learn' phase is not time-limited – it carries on for the rest of the children's lives. The books they now read contain a greater number of words than are in their oral language comprehension. Books now drive their vocabulary growth.

The simple view of writing

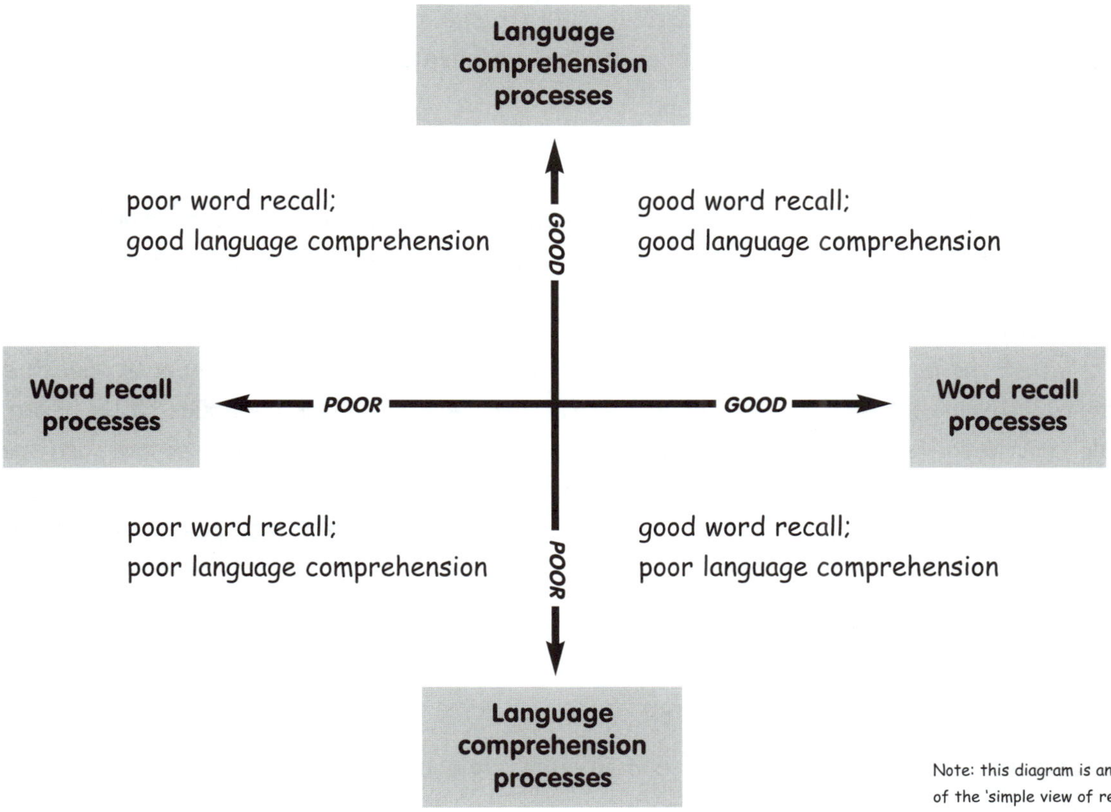

Note: this diagram is an adaptation of the 'simple view of reading'.

Children need to have both good word recall and good oral language comprehension in order to write. Good word recall is dependent upon encoding rapidly. Good oral language comprehension is dependent upon the deliberate use of talk.

As writers we need to encode rapidly before we can write even the simplest message. To write complex passages we need to encode easily so all our energy can go into writing down the message onto the page.

The 'learn to write (encode)' phase should also be time-limited; children should be out of this phase by the age of seven – albeit with 'phonically legal' spelling.

Teachers' emphasis upon children's oral language comprehension is also necessary for writing. The process of learning to read and write hand-in-hand, has a symbiotic relationship to the vocabulary growth needed for comprehension and composition. The more new words we read the more our vocabulary grows and our thinking develops. The creativity needed to write grows through reading widely and often.

1 Phonics: the route to good word recognition and recall

Phonics is the process by which speech is written down.

Speech sounds

Spoken words are formed by articulating groups of speech sounds.
Each speech sound, broadly speaking, is articulated with one mouth movement. In the words cat, chat, light and stay, for example, there are three mouth movements. In the words slip, stick, tent, flight, cloud, there are four mouth movements.
Each language has a different number of speech sounds. Finnish has 21, Spanish 24, Italian 27. English has about 44.
Although each language is spoken with different accents, most speech sounds are more or less consistent. In English, all but four or five of the 44 sounds are pronounced consistently across all accents.

Written sounds

The principle of the alphabetic writing system is to visually codify speech. Ideally each speech sound is represented with one letter. The writing system for European languages continues to be based on the roman alphabet with its 26 letters. The roman languages, with around 26 speech sounds, are spelt with just one of the 26 letters representing one sound – with only a few minor variations. This is called a 'simple' alphabetic code. Unsurprisingly, Italian and Spanish children learn to read and spell quickly and easily.

English, with its 44 speech sounds, has insufficient letters for each sound, so groups of letters have been combined to write the extra 18. To make it even harder, each sound is written down in more than one way! For example:

- The speech sound 'f' is spelt f, ff and ph.
- The speech sound 'ay' is spelt ay, ai, a-e, aigh, eigh, eig and ei!

This is called a complex alphabetic code. English has the most complicated code in the world. Children, learning to read in English, have over 150 graphemes (letter groups) to learn in order to read and spell the 44 speech sounds. No wonder they take longer to read and spell than Spanish and Italian children.

To make reading and writing easier for children, *Read Write Inc. Phonics* starts with a simple code – so children learn one way to read and write each of the 44 speech sounds. At this stage children read texts limited to 44 spellings. However they are able to write any word they can speak, albeit with the simple code, e.g. day, trayn, mayk; green, dreem, kee; blow, smowk, gowt.
They then quickly go on to read and write the other letters or groups of letters representing the same 44 speech sounds.
However, when children can read words like broccoli, accommodation, liaison, and independent, they will continue to make errors in spelling the same words, because of the range of alternatives in the English code.

Decoding

When we read a word, each letter or letter group (grapheme) triggers a speech sound. The speech sounds are then blended into a spoken word. This is called *decoding.*
The more we decode the same word, the sooner we recognise it 'on sight' and it becomes part of our orthographic store of words (this is the ability to read the word on sight, knowing at the same time its constituent sound-grapheme correspondences). The more words in our orthographic store, the quicker we read and our energy is freed for comprehension. When we decode a new word outside our lexicon, e.g. eucatastrophe – *and* we learn its pronunciation and meaning (a happy ending) – *and* we say and use the word out loud a few times, our orthographic store of words grows, and therefore the greater our vocabulary. The greater our vocabulary, the more books we can understand.

Encoding

When we write a word, we start with the spoken word. We segment the word into speech sounds and write the corresponding grapheme for each sound. This is called encoding. When we repeatedly encode a word, we recall the word sooner from our orthographic store.
Synthetic Phonics teaching is built upon the reversibility principle of the alphabetic code: we decode the graphemes into sounds in order to read and we encode sounds into graphemes to spell.

2 Talk: the route to good language comprehension

Hart and Risley (1995) found that there was a very tight link between the academic success of a child and the number of words the child's parents spoke to the child up to the age of three.

For children in homes where there is constant one-to-one chatter about things, people, characters, feelings and ideas, the parents deliberately build on what their children say every time they speak. 'Dog' grows to 'big dog' to 'huge shaggy alsation'. 'Bus' to 'red bus' to discussing the advantages of routemasters over bendy buses. Children talk, and ask questions – endlessly - and these parents build on what they say, until very soon these children are talking in elaborate and extended sentences. They keep up a constant commentary about every event in their children's lives. And they praise their children constantly. *Lovely darling!* These children have listened to over a thousand storytimes, know every nursery rhyme and fairy story by heart. They have been encouraged to ask questions: *What's that...? Who is that...? When...? Where...?* and mostly *Why...?*

These children already have an extensive vocabulary and, once they can read, they will not only know these words, but will then further extend their vocabulary through the new words they encounter in the books they read. They will still be asking the questions they have become accustomed to ask: *What does this mean? Why do you think...?* These are the children who have many ideas to write about – and vocabulary to draw upon. They are imaginative because they have imagined other worlds and places. They are creative because they have created scenarios and pictures through talk. *Daddy, what if dinosaurs were alive today...?* Parents have fed them more and more ideas and given them a love of language – and talking.

Most of school learning will be icing on the cake for these children. (As long as they learn to read.)
Others start school with a much lower level of language comprehension and knowledge of the world.
Although we cannot hope to emulate the constant one-to-one talk of the home environment above we can make a huge difference for these other children – if we use our time in carefully planned talk with our children. And not by using precious time observing them and collecting 'evidence' of their learning. No parent does this! The child is evidence enough.

Language enhances thought. So, however carefully planned the play activities, displays and 'experiences' – without deliberately planned talk the activity lacks meaning. You can feel the sand run though your fingers – but without words, it remains a sensual experience.

Only if we plan the talk, very deliberately, can we begin to close the gap. Numbers of children and shortage of time necessitate that in school, we plan more strategically than a parent. In the Foundation years, teachers and assistants need to lead small talking groups throughout the day, and in subsequent years plan constant discussion in every lesson using partner work and feedback. (See page 16, Developing language comprehension.)

The five principles 3

Read Write Inc. has five underlying principles – the five Ps.

1 Pace

Pace is key to the programme in two ways:
Firstly, for children to complete it as quickly as possible: to know the sounds thoroughly, but only to read as many books as necessary to learn to decode effortlessly.
Secondly, children should be so involved in the lesson that they do not have any 'down time'. This is not to say we want teachers to rush through the lesson – but for them to be energetic and rigorous.
To ensure no time is wasted, 'silent signals' are used to ensure quick, effective class management. They save the teacher from using her voice for low-level class management, shouting, shushing and nagging.

Silent signals

Silent stop signal
Hold a hand in the air (without clapping). Do not talk while your hand is raised. Children raise their hands in response and check their partner and others at the table have seen the signal, gently tapping an arm if necessary. If the signal fails, practise – *all* children should respond.

Magnet signal
Use when you need to check everyone is looking at you. Touch one finger on either side of your eyes. Their eyes should be fixed liked magnets on your eyes.

My turn, your turn signal (MTYT)
This is needed for choral work in the phonic lessons and the sound and word activities.
My turn: touch your chest with your palm
Your turn: open your palm to the children
Tell the children this is your signal and not theirs.

Perfect partner position signal
Teach children that when you run your hand down your opposite arm, it is a signal for them to sit side-by-side ready to talk to their partners.

1, 2, 3
These allow you to move the children from one place to another, quickly.
For example, from the carpet to their tables:
Hold up one finger: children stand
Two fingers: walk and stand behind chairs
Three fingers: sit down and prepare to read

2 Praise – a lot

Children learn more quickly when they are praised for what they do well, rather than nagged for what they do wrong; catch children displaying the behaviour you need for learning to be successful – particularly praising effective partner work. Always praise the teaching partners for their effective teaching.

Praise phrases
Use 'praise phrases' for the teaching partner to acknowledge impressive partner work (and to grow positive vocabulary).
Examples: super/ smashing/ brilliant sounds/ sentences; fantastic/ fabulous/ phenomenal Fred Talk; wondrous/ wonderful/ wicked words; remarkable/ rapid reading/ writing

Praise actions
Use *praise actions* to keep the children energetic and to praise excellent behaviour and hard work.
Examples: high five/ thumbs up; fireworks and whooshes (act out); *Go guys!* (circle thumbs); Elvis (thank you, thank you, thank you very much – push hand though hair); marshmallow claps (squishy clap); microwaves (little finger waves)

3 Purpose

Each activity in the programme has a very clear purpose. The teacher sets the purpose at the beginning of each activity so the children fully understand what they are learning and why.
The purpose of the teaching is made clear through *modelling* and *thinking out loud.*

Modelling
The teacher models, with a child or another adult, the behaviour needed for effective partner work: partner discussion and partner teaching. Assemblies are good times, by acting out with the children and staff, to show the expectations for partner teaching, partner discussion and feedback mechanisms.

Think out loud
Thinking out loud is a device used to *show* the thinking necessary to an activity. It is used in all the comprehension and compositional activities.
It is *planned* chatter to let children 'see' what we think; as if having a thinking bubble coming out of our heads. It is used to show them how we make decisions about what characters are thinking, saying and feeling and what is going on in the story, or how we decide the best word to write.
Don't make it look too easy! Hesitate as you *think out loud.* Ask *yourself* questions and answer them *yourself.*

4 Participation

Participation is key to the programme. *All* children take part in *all* of the lesson.
Full participation is gained through choral work – *My turn, your turn* – and partner work.

My turn, your turn
This is used when you need the children to copy. Children should always sit where they can see your mouth and eyes easily, and you theirs – whether they are sitting on the carpet or at tables.

Partner work
Partner work is deeply embedded in the programme because:
✯ We learn and retain so much more when we discuss a question or problem with someone else.

☆ We only really know that we know something when we teach it to someone else.

If you don't have consistent partner work, only a few children talk in the lesson – the one or two children who are selected from the confident 20% of children who do raise their hands to reply. In other words, only 6% of children answer the question intended for 100%. Children who are not expected to participate switch off.

Once your partner work is established thoroughly throughout the day, 'hands-up' becomes an anathema to good teaching.

Partnerships

Organise new partnerships about every four weeks. You will need to model effective partner behaviour for a long time until it becomes a habit. Model how the children should sit – shoulder-to-shoulder. Always praise children for working co-operatively.

Quick 'bonding' activities help new partner relationships, e.g. 'I know all about my partner': partners find out their partner's favourite food, TV programme, film, computer game, story and what makes them cross, irritated, happy...

Some partnerships are more successful than others, but stick in there – if you take it seriously, they will too. The alternative is reverting to hands-up and low participation. Praise good partner work throughout the day, until it becomes 'what you do'.

Possible partnerships

Pair two assertive children – let them battle it out!

Pair two shy children – someone has to talk!

Mix boys and girls, first and second language learners.

Partner teaching

Partner teaching is used to ensure that children can do and understand what you have taught them; children may appear to understand within the group, but you will only know if they really know when they can teach each other. It is your time to assess the effectiveness of your teaching!

Many children get so good at teaching their partners that they also teach their siblings to read at home. It gives children a strong sense that 'they know what they know'. Independence increases and self esteem flourishes.

Partner teaching is used for sound and word reading activities 1, 2 and 9 in the Storybook lessons. However, use it throughout the whole day in every curriculum area – it is your key assessment tool.

Model

Model every day (if briefly later), with another child. Show the children how *and* what to teach.

Tell the children who is Partner 1 or 2 (or Red/Green or Tom/Jerry). Ask teaching partners to hold the teaching stick (a lolly stick) for pointing under the sounds or words their partner reads.

Move around the partners, praising them for their good pointing, and good helping – spotting and praising successful teaching, and checking that teaching partners correct every error. If not, explain the point they have missed and get them to re-teach it. Never intervene and teach the reading partner. You have given the 'teacher' a job to do, and he needs to learn to do it.

Model how teaching partners praise their partners, using 'praise phrases': 'Good job! Super sounds! Wicked words.'

Praise the teaching partners for good pointing and helping – a lot!

Ask teaching partners to praise reading partners: 'Brilliant sounds!' or 'Excellent words', 'Fabulous Fred Talk'.

Turn to your partner – discussion

Partnership discussion is used in the Ditty and Storybook lessons 3, 5, 6, 8 to ensure children understand the story, vocabulary and ideas and writing activities 6, 7 and 8 to grow ideas and compose sentences.

Partner behaviour

Model the behaviour needed for effective discussion. Use assembly times, when all the teachers can model with a partner (showily!) how they discuss questions asked by the assembly leader.
Model how you want children to:

- repeat the question (mostly)
- talk loud enough but not too loudly
- take turns in talking
- listen to each other
- build on what their partner says
- say 'we think' or 'my partner thinks, but I think...'
- stop with the signal

Praise children for their excellent partner work, and show them why what they did was so effective – to act as models to others.

Feedback

After children have turned to their partners to answer a question, take feedback in four main ways:

1. 'Choose Two': select two children to share their answers.
   Do not choose hand raisers – they will still try to take over!
2. 'Paraphrase': rephrase a child's answer.
3. 'Choral': ask children to show thumbs up or down, if the answer is short and needs only a yes/no or a one or two word response.
4. 'Popcorn': ask children to call out their answers – when the answer is short with many different answers, e.g. give me angry words!

Listen carefully as they respond, build upon the idea, say it back and then get the children to repeat your phrase or sentence.

5 Passion

Be passionate in your teaching. Show the children how much you love teaching the lessons. Exaggerate your modelling of thinking and behaviour. Make your teaching larger than life so children engage in the learning. The greater the passion, the faster their progress!

Developing language comprehension

Language comprehension is developed within and alongside the RWI lessons by building sentences together in carefully planned talk throughout the day in four key ways:

1. Build a sentence
2. Talk through the day
3. Talk through play
4. Talk through story and rhymes

1 Build a sentence – orally

Thinking about vocabulary in four layers helps plan the talk we use strategically.

- *First layer words* are those children are most likely to know, e.g. happy, sad, angry, run, walk, eat.
- *Second layer words* are synonymous with first layer words but refined for particular circumstances, e.g. cheerful, miserable, furious, race, dawdle, munch, slurp.
- *Third layer words* are those in storybooks that we, as adults, don't often use in everyday speech, e.g. jocular, melancholy, apoplectic, promenade as well as language particular to a genre or historical period: once upon a time, venturing out, what ails thee, languishing.
- *Fourth layer words* are subject specific, e.g. intestines, stegosaurus, evaporate, stem.

(This idea is adapted from Isobel Beck's three tiers of vocabulary concept.)
Plan to use second layer vocabulary throughout the day, consciously and deliberately. Build upon what children say and help them differentiate and refine their understanding of everything that is, for example, 'dog'.
Show real objects, pictures, interactive whiteboard illustrations and storybooks of dogs.
Use *My turn, your turn* to get children to repeat. Build up to three adjectives.
First layer words to describe 'dog' could include: big/ small, black/ brown, shiny/ rough, nasty/ nice, fat/ thin.
Use silly voices to match the words you use. Let the children see you *think out loud* as you decide the words. 'Dog... Big dog... Big black dog... Big black shiny dog... A big black shiny dog is sitting on the rug.'
Second layer words to describe 'dog' could include: massive/ minute, jet-black/ russet, glossy/ matted, fierce/ welcoming, skinny/ pudgy, and alsation/ poodle.
'Dog... Massive dog... Massive fierce dog... *A massive fierce dog is barking at the gate.*'

As children's vocabulary grows use humour and irony. For example, show a picture of a sweet little dog. 'Nasty big fierce dog, grrrrrrr! Help! A huge fierce dog is chasing me.'

As children's language develops start to ask more open questions until, as a group, you build stories together orally. Get all the children to say the sentences out loud at each stage as you build, using *My turn, your turn*. Take ideas from the children and feed in your own too, e.g. use a picture of a wet dog or draw a simple sketch.
Ask: 'What did the owner shout to the dog?' TTYP and feed back, e.g. No! You are filthy.
Mrs Brown shouted "Oh no, you naughty dog!"
'Was she furious or amused?' Furious
Furiously, Mrs Brown shouted at her dog "You naughty dog!"
'What did the dog look like?' Wet/ drippy/ soaking/ bedraggled/ forlorn (feed in) ears down
Furiously, Mrs Brown shouted at her bedraggled dog. His ears drooped when she shouted "You naughty dog!"
The story could develop...
"No – not the carpet!" she screamed as Driver dashed through the front door spraying the remains of the muddy puddle on Mrs Brown's new white carpet.
Children develop their vocabulary, ability to construct sentences and their knowledge of the world through assistance and repetition. The children must say the words out loud many times, in different situations, so they start to 'own' the words.

Develop stories using objects
For example, Sam holds a favourite object: an old teddy
Teacher: 'Sam has a brown teddy'. (Children repeat.) 'Are the teddy's eyes gleamy or dull?' TTYP.
'What has happened to the left eye?' TTYP.
Teacher *thinks out loud* using children's suggestions: 'Sam has a brown teddy with only one eye. No, let me build on that: *Sam's poor teddy has only one beady eye, and it's dangling on a string!'*
Children repeat chorally, a couple of times.
Teacher: 'Tell your partner about the teddy's fur.'
Choose two for feedback: scruffy/ no hair
Teacher: 'Yes, it's very scruffy and worn. Sam – were you a little baby when you were given this teddy?'
Sam: 'No, it was Mummy's, when she was little.'
Teacher: 'You must both love the teddy so much – I can tell this because he is so worn out from cuddling.'
Teacher *thinks out loud*: 'Let me think of another sentence about Sam's teddy. So far we have...
Sam's poor teddy has only one beady eye, and that's dangling on a string!
He has been cuddled so much that he is... scruffy... no, let's say shabby and worn.'
Children repeat the sentence and then try to say both!
The children cannot encode yet, but they can compose – with your assistance.

Once children start to write, the same activity can be used to support their composition.
Although the children can say the elaborate sentence, only model writing some of the sentence.
As the children's encoding develops, model writing more of what they say out loud, until they can encode all of the sentence they can say out loud.
All children can write – if you help build their ideas orally first.

2 Talk through the day

Give children a choice of words so they use one of the words in their reply. If we ask a child how he's feeling, he will say 'happy' or 'sad'. If we ask him if he's feeling very miserable or just a little miserable, he will use the word 'miserable' in his reply, and learn to use different gradations of sadness in different situations.
I'm not just cross that you have hit Lucas, I am furious! How am I feeling?
Furious.
Yes furious!
Let me see, shall we clomp or creep into the hall? Let's creep so we don't disturb anyone and then we can clomp! The children whisper creep, creep, creep as they walk, and say stomp, stomp, stomp as they march.
Dawdle, dawdle, I need you to hurry, hurry. Children are asked to repeat.
Mrs Smith, you are looking very elegant today in your new dress. Children, tell Mrs Smith how elegant she looks!
You must be exhausted from running about. Are you feeling exhausted or are you going to dash about again?
Is that pear crunchy or squashy?
Does the glue feel slimy or sticky?

Open the question, only when you know that children have the words to choose between. *How does this music make you feel?* If they say sad/happy (and they will, to begin with) probe further!

Feed children with 'second layer' words. Be ambitious. Language development takes planning – day-by-day and year-by-year. It does not just evolve. Explain to parents and older children what you are doing so they can use these words at home. Get dinner ladies involved – *Do you want the mushy potatoes, crunchy carrots and spicy curry or would you like...?*

3 Talk through play

Before children play

In the Foundation years ensure children 'choose' all activities so they have full access to the language associated with all areas of learning, as well as practising encoding and decoding skills.

Plan the second layer words, the extended sentences and the way you will build the children's sentences with the staff, so they also use this vocabulary as they move around the room. Say the words with the children before they get there so that when they do they are more likely to use the words. Build upon the words and sentences day-by-day, week-by-week.

For example:

Play dough: 'Mmmm don't you love *forcing* your hands into the play dough: squishy squashy, squish, squash... Let's say *Force my hands in – squish, squash, squish, squash.*'

Get children to repeat the words in silly voices – low, high, like a giant, witch, fairy.

Mud: (pretending) 'Let's squeeze mud through our fingers: squelchy, welchy, yucky mmm... Let's say *Squeeze the mud through my fingers – squelchy, welchy, yucky mmmm.*'

Water: 'I've got a windmill that whizzes water – spray goes everywhere, sprinkle, froth and foam, sprinkle, froth, foam... Let's say *Whizz the windmill – sprinkle froth foam.*'

Bikes: 'We have a new speedy bike. It whizzes and whirls you like a firework. Let's say...'

While children are playing

Pin the words on Post-its (small for the teacher next to each activity to ensure they are used). When the children can read the words, add them to your Power Words Wall.

Plan for all staff to use these words, and to encourage the children to use them during the play. Make up chants that you can say with the children while they play:

I love mud. We love mud. We all love mud.
Thick and squishy.
Squishy wishy squelchy welchy mud.
I love mud. We love mud.

After playing

After children have been playing, choose one play area to build upon the words and phrases, e.g. choose a child who has been playing in the doctor's surgery.

Teacher: 'Dr Khan, who's been poorly today?'

'Sam'

Teacher: 'Oh no, what's wrong?'

'Sam's got a poorly leg.'

Teacher: 'How did he get it?'

'He fell off his bike.'

Teacher: '*Sam has a poorly leg because he fell off his bike.*'

Ask children to repeat.

Teacher: 'How did you treat him?'

'I put a bandage on.'
Teacher: '*Dr Khan put a bandage on Sam's poorly leg.*'
Ask the children to repeat.

After painting
Discuss a child's picture.
Teacher: 'Let's talk about Virdauda's picture... What are the colours you've used?'
'Black and blue and white.'
'Virdauda's painting is... dark and sploshy with bits of white gleaming through.'

Keep full participation by getting all the children to repeat your sentences. Do not use a circle – when each child takes it in turn to speak one-by-one, each child speaks very little.

4 Talk through story and rhymes

Decide, as a school, the nursery rhymes, finger rhymes, poetry and songs that you want the children to know by heart, term-by term, year-by-year. Leave nothing to chance.
Plan storytimes with rigour! Story not only develops children's vocabulary but also their understanding of the human condition by talking about characters and their motives; e.g. opposing forces of right and wrong, good and evil, wise and foolish. It also develops their imagination by conjuring up strange and wonderful places, lands, characters, feelings and actions.

Decide the fairy stories, traditional tales, myths and fables and stories by famous authors that you want your children to be able to retell. Choose these carefully so that you have a canon of stories that you will read to the children again and again over the years. Start in the Foundation years and build up a collection of stories – about fifteen a year – you will read to the children over and over so they get to know them very well. This is over and above all the other picture books you read to them.

Plan the story readings so you can read with carefully considered pace and expression.
Select the second and third layer vocabulary – in particular, words to explain emotion, movement, speech and the senses. Build an ever-increasing vocabulary – grown from these carefully selected texts – and use this vocabulary through the day. When the children can read the words, add them to your Power Word Wall.

Show the children how much you enjoy the phrases as you explain their meanings.
Say the phrases with expression and intonation that gives further meaning to the phrases.
Let the children enjoy the stories, and when they know them really well, use 'talk about' questions, e.g.
What if?
What if the king wasn't a good kind king, but a wicked nasty person?
What if it wasn't a frog, but a bear?
What if the witch had been kind, and not mean?

Dramatic reconstruction
Put all the children into role as one character. Use TTYP and quick feedback to ask them questions. Build on their answers using second and third layer vocabulary, and then ask all the children to repeat your sentence, chorally. Build up the sentences into longer sentences, getting them to repeat the sentence out loud. Show the children how you have to think hard to construct your sentences – don't make it look too easy! Hesitate so children jump in while you (pretend) to think. Model how you repeat the sentences to check if it sounds correct.

Give the children alternative words, so they say the word out loud, e.g. to Goldilocks:
Question 1: 'Why did you go into the bears' cottage?'
Take feedback, e.g. Tired/ hungry.
'So you were hungry – and exhausted too. Lets all say... *I was hungry and exhausted.*'
Think out loud: 'Let me think... I know: *I was hungry and exhausted... I was so hungry and exhausted that I went into the bears' cottage to see what I could find.*
Let's all say... *I was so hungry and exhausted that I crept into the bears' cottage to see if I could find something to eat.'*
Repeat until children can say the whole sentence – emphasising particular words.

Question 2: 'So what did you hope to find to eat when you went in there?' Cornflakes/ toast...
'Did you feel disappointed or pleased when you saw the porridge?' Disappointed.
'Show me how you looked – you do look disappointed! Your faces look all grumpy.'
Think out loud: 'Let me see... When I saw it was porridge on the table, I was very disappointed.'
Ask children to repeat.
'Why did you try three lots of porridge? So the first was too hot. Did it burn your tongue? Let's all say: *The porridge was so hot, it burnt my tongue.'*
Repeat for the other bowls of porridge. Add your own voices.
When telling stories add extra voices – 'shrieked Goldilocks'/ 'whined little bear'.

The headteacher

When the headteacher works with the staff to ensure that every child learns to read, children make quicker progress. Teaching in, what is likely to be a new and different way, can take time to master. Schools will achieve the most when all the staff - headteacher, teachers, and support staff, have been trained.

RWI headteachers need to:

- attend the initial two-day training
- release their RWI manager for at least three hours a week to work with RWI staff and children
- set key reading targets with the manager (see below).

RWI 'model' schools welcome visits from schools and are keen to share their good practice. See www.readwriteinc.com

RWI manager

The manager's role is critical. Once staff have received the two-day training, bought the resources and grouped the children, the work of the manager really begins. The RWI manager, with the headteacher, should drive RWI, ensuring it is taught with fidelity so that all children complete the programme as quickly as possible. The manager needs to be an experienced teacher, well organised and above all, have the ability to persevere until *every* child can read.

The manager needs time to do this properly. In schools where there are many children learning to read, the manager should support and model lessons in three RWI sessions a week. In very big schools, the manager should work with reading teachers in every RWI session.

The manager has three main roles:

1. to ensure children are making good progress in the 'lower progress' groups and organise one-to-one tutoring for those children who need extra support.
2. to keep all the groups at the same homogeneous reading level (by regularly checking groups).
3. to *show* how the programme should be taught to the reading teachers, in assemblies, demonstrating lessons to groups of reading teachers.

RWI reading teachers

RWI reading teachers should be made up of a team of good teachers and TAs (teaching assistants) who each teach a group of children at the same reading level.

TAs should teach small groups of four to eight - unless an HTL has a special arrangement with the headteacher to teach more.

Reading teachers need to alert the manager to any child whose progress is either faster or slower than the rest of the group.

One-to-one tutors

Children in the 'lowest' attaining group have the widest variety of needs and are therefore the least homogeneous group of all. In order that these children can receive the same carefully targeted RWI teaching as all the other groups of children, some may need one-to-one tutoring for 10 to 20 minutes a day - on top of their group session in the morning. (See page 92, one-to-one tutoring.)

The RWI manager will need to train between two and five one-to-one tutors, depending upon the size of the school and the mobility of children.

Individual special needs assistants should also be trained to work with the children they support. The headteacher should select assistants from their *existing staff* who have a total commitment and a genuine passion for teaching children to read.

It is particularly effective when senior teachers, without class responsibility, including the headteacher, tutor at least one child. This sends a strong message to staff and parents – this school is serious about getting every child to read.

These tutors will become 'real' experts in the skills of teaching reading to challenging children, therefore benefiting *all* the children they work with throughout the day.

Attendance manager

The programme is intensive and cumulative, so poor attendance would severely disrupt a child's progress. The RWI attendance manager, usually a TA, needs to arrange a meeting with the RWI manager or headteacher and the parents of the children who have poor attendance *and* low reading ability. The attendance manager phones parents at 8.30 a.m. to check the child is on his way to school. A suggested letter to parents for you to adapt as necessary is provided below.

Dear Mr and Mrs Smith,

Tom's reading

Tom is about to take part in a very intensive reading and writing programme. He will also receive extra tutoring every day. We want to do everything we can to make sure that your son learns to read.

We need your help though!

If Tom is to receive all this extra support he must come to school **every** day at 9.00, unless he is *very* poorly. We are happy to help you do this by phoning you every morning at 8.30 to check Tom is up and ready for school.

Please could you sign the form below if you agree to help.

Mrs Jones, the reading manager would like to meet you to discuss all the work we are about to do with Tom on 3rd May at 3.15 when you pick up Tom from school.

Best wishes

Headteacher

....

I agree to help Tom learn to read by making sure he arrives at school every day at 9.00.

Mr and Mrs Smith

Training, implementation and support

The two-day RWI training is essential if the school is serious about getting every child to read. When every teacher and teaching assistant is trained to teach a child to read and write, particularly the headteacher, you can eradicate illiteracy from your school.

After the training, arrange an Implementation Monitoring day with an RWI trainer so she can spend the day with the headteacher and RWI manager, observing and monitoring and importantly, showing lessons and one-to-one tutoring sessions.

Many schools book further support days each year to keep up to date with new developments.
New staff to the school can be trained on one of the central trainings – see www.ruthmiskinliteracy.com

How to get started

This is a shorthand guide to implementing *Read Write Inc. Phonics.*

Book the training

See www.ruthmiskinliteracy.com

Before the training

- Choose an RWI manager – the manager may want to go on a central training course before the rest of the school is trained
- Manager organises staff meeting. (See page 24.)
- Manager orders RWI resources. Phone an Oxford University Press Representative to help you – they have been fully trained on *Read Write Inc.* and have a thorough knowledge of the programme. See www.readwriteinc.com
- All staff have the two-day training – make sure everybody is there, especially the headteacher.

After the training

Week 1

- Manager assesses all children using Sound and Word Entry Assessment (see page 28) and records results in the Assessment Tracker grid (see page 30.)
- Manager organises children into broad Speed Sounds groups for 30 minutes a day for four weeks. (Do not start Storybook lessons.)
- Manager checks all teaching areas have the materials for the Speed Sounds lessons.
- Manager holds Staff Meetings 1 and 2 (see page 24).

Weeks 2, 3, 4 and 5

- Teachers of Year 1 (P2) and higher (to Year 6 [P7] if necessary) start Speed Sounds lessons – 30 minutes a day. YR (P1) teacher – 15–20 minutes a day.
- Teachers aim to get children to know as many sound-grapheme correspondences over these four weeks as possible.
- Manager trains the one-to-one tutors, and decides the children who will be tutored. (See page 92.)

Week 6

- Speed Sounds groups stop; class teachers continue with best-fit lessons for one week.
  RWI manager:
  Assesses the children again using the Sound and Word Asssessments and the story reading, if necessary. (See page 32.)

- Re-groups the children into new homogeneous groups – not including herself in the groups. (See page 33).
- Re-enters the children onto an Assessment Tracker grid (see page 30).
- Gives out RWI Storybook resources for new groups.
- Holds Staff Meeting 3.

Week 7

- Full programme begins: one-hour sessions in Years 1–6 (P2–P7). Reception (P1) continue with 15–20 minutes.
- Children go into new homogeneous groups with their new reading teacher.
  Reading teachers teach both Speed Sounds lessons + Ditty + Storybook lessons
  RWI Manager checks all the groups are OK – encourages and helps (See implementation checklist at www.readwriteinc.com.)
- RWI Manager holds Staff Meeting 4.

Weeks 8–12

RWI manager:

- Models teaching in lowest progress groups to ensure that teachers are very secure.
- Checks on children being tutored every week.
- Holds review meeting with one-to-one tutors (see page 92.)
- Pops in and out of groups every day, modelling lessons - encouraging and helping.
- Holds Staff Meeting 5 on Storybook lessons and writing lessons (see below).

Week 13 +

RWI manager:

- Swaps roles with a very good teacher (for four weeks), so she has the chance to teach the programme.
- Frees other reading teachers to observe each other.
- Continues to ensure all teachers are teaching the programme to the highest level.
- Continues to check the slowest children are making excellent progress.
- Continues to hold Staff Meetings.

First staff meetings – following RWI training

Plan to hold staff meetings every week for the first term.

Staff Meeting 1

- Check everyone knows the equipment they need for the Speed Sounds lessons.
- Practise teaching Speed Sounds Set 1 and blending: decide how, as a staff group, you will make sure every child learns this quickly.
- Plan the implementation of storytimes (See page 19.)

Staff Meeting 2

- Practise teaching Speed Sounds Set 2 and 3: explain how to whizz children through the programme when they know Set 2 sounds.

Staff Meeting 3

- Check everyone knows how to the teach the Speed Sounds lessons alongside the Ditty/ Storybook lessons.

Staff Meeting 4

- The Ditties: discuss how to make these effective and fun.

Staff Meeting 5

- Reading activities 1, 2, and 9 (sound and word level): discuss how the activities build to support reading activity 4.

Staff Meeting 6

- Reading activities 3, 6 and 7 (understanding the text): discuss how the activities grow vocabulary and ideas that feed into the writing activities.

Staff Meeting 7

- Writing activities 1, 2, 3 and 4 (spelling): discuss how these link back to the phonic lessons.

Staff Meeting 8

- Writing activities 6, 8 and 9 (composition): discuss how to plan these lessons.

Staff Meeting 9

- Discuss marking, editing, celebrating and displaying children's writing.

Staff Meeting 10

- Discuss effectiveness of partner work – no hands up!

Staff Meeting 11

- Examine the impact of the 5 Ps on lessons through the rest of the curriculum.

There is a DVD and workbook of all lessons available for schools to buy after whole school training. See www.ruthmiskinliteracy.com

The manager, based on the progress of teaching, will determine future monthly meetings.

Keep an RWI whiteboard in the staffroom where reading teachers can write questions and offer ideas.

Initial assessment

Assess all children, who are reading below Level 3, on the Sound and Word Entry Assessment on page 28. Children who are reading at Level 3 and above are better placed on *RWI Spelling* with *RWI Comprehension.*

1. Identify the nonsense words and explain that they are 'silly' words. (Otherwise children read them incorrectly by trying to force the pronunciation into a real word.) Some children can read words 'on sight' without being able to sound-blend the words. Nonsense words are used to check that all children can sound-blend new words and syllables.
2. Children read **from the top** of the chart.
3. When the child is unable to read further, go back to the box the child can read completely. Find the equivalent level on the Sound and Word Entry Assessment Placement Chart on page 29, to see where the child should start on the programme.
4. Use the Assessment Tracker on page 30 to track children's progress.

Notes on assessment

- The assessments are cumulative. Children must read from the top of the chart each time. This will ensure there are no gaps in their knowledge of sounds.
- Do not worry if their sounds are not pure when reading the first set of sounds - many teachers do not use pure sounds before the training!
- If you are unsure whether the child will be able to cope with a particular level, ask the child to read a couple of pages from a book at the given level. If the child reads too slowly, consider placing him on the level below.
- Early stage EAL children who have good decoding skills should read the Yellow, Blue and Grey Storybooks, before starting *RWI Comprehension.*

Weeks 1–4

Once you have carried out the initial assessment, organise teachers to teach the children in broadly homogeneous phonic groups – mixing children from different years, if necessary.

Teach these groups for the first four weeks – just for 30 minutes a day, with teaching assistants observing so they can practise with the teachers – ready for when they have their own groups. The aim of these four weeks is for children to learn to read as many sounds as possible on cards and in words. Although children are taught to write the sounds and words, emphasis is placed hugely on reading them.

At the end of the four weeks, re-assess the children using Sound and Word Assessment 2 (see page 32) and place them on a new grid, keeping the original starting place and date next to their name to show progress.
Group the children homogeneously, mixing year groups where necessary.

There is a third Sound and Word Assessment provided on page 34. This is because children will be assessed regularly during the programme so it is important to alternate tests to ensure that they do not start to memorise them.

Every eight weeks

1. Reassess the children using Sound and Word Assessments 2 and 3, (rotate regularly to provide variety) recording the data on the Assessment Tracker.
2. Re-group the children

The aim of RWI Phonics is for children to complete the programme as quickly as possible. The sooner they complete the phonic programme the sooner they will be able to choose books to read at their own interest and comprehension level. It is vital that children go at the pace of their own decoding ability. The stories are explained to the children so those with poor comprehension have equal access to them. Remember the children are grouped homogeneously according to reading. Their writing is judged by outcome - to allow for the difference in children's encoding and handwriting ability.
So, given that the aim of the programme is to finish it - quick learners read fewer books than slower learners!

Foundation Stage organisation

Reception grouping

Term 1

Speed Sounds lessons and Word Time! (see page 37)

- Teach children the Set 1 Speed Sounds and Word Time!, as a whole class, for around six weeks. Then split the class into groups according to the progress they have made.
- The teacher has the largest group for 15-20 minutes. The teaching assistant has the smaller group for 15-20 minutes. *Or* the teacher takes both groups in succession.
- Organise extra small group work for six to seven minutes at the appropriate level:
  - speeding up the reading of Set 1 Speed Sounds
  - using magnetic letters for blending
  - rereading the Ditties or Storybooks.

Term 2

- Group children, according to reading progress, across the Reception classes for 30 minutes a day.
- Allocate a teacher or assistant to each group. Or the teacher takes groups in succession.
- Teach the Speed Sound lessons for 15 minutes, then text level work (Word Time!, Ditties or Storybook) for 15 minutes.

Term 3

- Continue as for Term 2 but for 30-40 minutes a day.
- At least half of the children should be on the Storybooks by now.
- Consider some more advanced children working with Year 1 (P2) children.

Sound and Word Entry Assessment

A	m a s d t i n p g o c k u b f e l h r j v y w v x z
B	sad fan tap map cup bid run hen gep rop baf lid ved
C	sh th ch qu ng nk shop chip rush thin ring sink quan losh chup ling thip
D	splosh thick hand dress click scomp poll stoff pand plick
E	ay ee igh ow oo oo play sleep flight blow spoon shook
F	ar or air ir ou oy part horse fair whirl shout toy
G	night round joy chair girl hard slorf slair flarf snay stoon trow ploun gleep
H	a-e i-e o-e ea shake pipe smoke clean pake jike doke feap
I	u-e ai oa ew oi ire ear er aw ow ure are ur slain float shrew spoil fire hear her claw brown pure share burn rude scur gloip slaw gler scear plare clowp smire skew scroap bluke graip hure
J	complain delay mistake disagree recognise tomorrow continue remark disappoint inspire admire attention delicious

Sound and Word Entry Assessment Placement Chart

	Sound and Word Assessment	Degree of sound blending used	Speed sounds to teach and review
A	No or few sounds	No blending	Teach Set 1 sounds Word Time! 1, 2, 3
B	m a s d t i n p g o c k u b f e l h r j v y w v x z sad fan tap map cup bid run hen gep rop baf lid ved	Needs to sound out most real and nonsense words	Review Set 1 sounds (Focus upon th, sh, ch, ck) Review Word Time! 1, 2, 3 Teach Word Time! 4, 5
C	sh th ch qu ng nk shop chip rush thin ring sink quan losh chup ling thip	Needs to sound out most real and nonsense words	Review Set 1 sounds Review Word Time! 1-5 Teach Word Time! 6, 7
D	splosh thick hand dress click scomp roll stoff pand plick	Can read 6 B-D *real* words *without* sound blending	Review Set 1 sounds Review Word Time! 1-7 Teach Set 2 sounds: ay, ee igh, ow, oo, oo
E	ay ee igh ow oo oo play sleep flight blow spoon shook	Can read 12 B-E *real* words *without* sound blending	Review Set 2 sounds: ay, ee, igh, ow, oo, oo Teach Set 2: ar, or, air, ir, ou, oy
F	ar or air ir ou oy part horse fair whirl shout toy	Can read most B-F *real* words *without* sound blending	Review Set 1 and 2 sounds Teach letter names
G	night round joy chair girl hard slorf slair flarf snay stoon trow ploun gleep	Can read most B-G *real* words *without* sound blending	Review Sets 1 and 2 sounds Teach Set 3: a-e i-e o-e ea
H	a-e i-e o-e ea shake pipe smoke clean pake jike doke feap	Can read most B-H *real* words *without* sound blending	Review Set 2 and Set 3 sounds a-e i-e o-e ea Teach rest of Set 3 sounds
I	u-e ai oa ew oi ire ear er aw ow ure are ur slain float shrew spoil fire hear her claw brown pure share burn rude scur gloip slaw gler scear plare clowp smire skew scroap bluke graip hure	Can read most B-I *real* words *without* sound blending	Review Sets 2 and 3 sounds
J	complain delay mistake disagree recognise tomorrow continue remark disappoint inspire admire attention delicious	Can read most B-J *real* words *without* sound blending	Child can progress on to *RWI Spelling*

Assessment Tracker

	YR	Y1	Y2	Y3	Y4
A					
B					
C					
D					
E					
F					
G					
H					
I					
J					

See page 31 for an example of how to use this record.

Example charts

Assessment Tracker – 4th September

	YR	Y1	Y2	Y3	Y4
A					
B		Lily Sunesh	Jack		
C		John, Sam Eva	Ada Max		
D		Rani	Erin, Katie		
E			Miya, Daniel		
F					
G					
H					
I					
J					

Assessment Tracker – 5th November

	YR	Y1	Y2	Y3	Y4
A					
B					
C					
D		Lily (B, 4/9/09), Sunesh (B, 4/9/09)	Jack (B, 4/9/09), Tom, (D, 5/11/09)		
E		John (C, 4/9/09) Eva (C, 4/9/09)	Ada (C, 4/9/09) Max (C, 4/9/09)		
F		Sam (C, 4/9/09), Rani (D, 4/9/09),	Erin (D, 4/9/09), Katie (D, 4/9/09)		
G			Miya (E, 4/9/09), Daniel (E, 4/9/09)		
H					
I					
J					

Write the starting place of each child on the first Assessment Tracker grid. On the subsequent grid, John may have moved to level E, but put the initial level and date in brackets after the name, to help track the speed of progress. The initial level and date should remain in brackets after the child's name for each subsequent grid.

Sound and Word Assessment 2

A	m a s d t i n p g o c k u b f e l h r j v y w v x z
B	bed net hat cog jug jam pot lip zop vem fas bip kug rab
C	sh th ch qu ng nk rink sing thick mush chin shop thop jing chib hish shap
D	pluck splash land press stick flump boll criff dimp blick
E	ay ee igh ow oo oo tray creep sight blow broom look
F	ar or air ir ou oy cart sport chair girl mouse toy
G	sight blouse boy hair dirt shark corf jair tarf zay ploop plow yout feen
H	a-e i-e o-e ea flame slime broke steam bame fibe chope gean
I	u-e ai oa ew oi ire ear er aw ow ure are ur plain moan flew joint hire fear her paw clown pure care purse flute flur sloip graw per grear splare flowp frew stoan vuke slaig ture
J	complaint holiday yesterday operate delight decide provoke pollute pronounce prepare argue surround annoy addition suspicious

Sound and Word Assessment 2 Placement Chart

	Sound and Word Assessment	Degree of sound blending used	Speed sounds to teach and review	Ditties or Storybooks
A	No or few sounds	No blending	Teach Set 1 sounds Word Time! 1, 2, 3	
B	m a s d t i n p g o c k u b f e l h r j v y w v x z bed net hat cog jug jam pot lip zop vem fas bip kug rab	Needs to sound out most real and nonsense words	Review Set 1 sounds (Focus upon th, sh, ch, ck) Review Word Time! 1, 2, 3 Teach Word Time! 4, 5	Ditties 1–20
C	sh th ch qu ng nk rink sing thick mush chin shop thop jing chib hish shap	Needs to sound out most real and nonsense words	Review Set 1 sounds Review Word Time! 1–5 Teach Word Time! 6, 7	Ditties 21+
D	pluck splash land press stick flump boll criff dimp blick	Can read 6 B-D *real* words *without* sound blending	Review Set 1 sounds Review Word Time! 1–7 Teach Set 2 sounds: ay, ee, igh, ow, oo, oo	Green Purple
E	ay ee igh ow oo oo tray creep sight blow broom look	Can read 12 B-E *real* words *without* sound blending	Review Set 2 sounds: ay, ee, igh, ow, oo, oo Teach Set 2: ar, or, air, ir, ou, oy	Pink
F	ar or air ir ou oy cart sport chair girl mouse toy	Can read most B-F *real* words *without* sound blending	Review Set 1 and 2 sounds Teach letter names	Orange
G	sight blouse boy hair dirt shark corf jair tarf zay ploop plow yout feen	Can read most B-G *real* words *without* sound blending	Review Set 1 and 2 sounds Teach Set 3: a-e i-e o-e ea	Yellow
H	a-e i-e o-e ea flame slime broke steam bame fibe chope gean	Can read most B-H *real* words *without* sound blending	Review Set 2 and Set 3 sounds a-e i-e o-e ea Teach rest of Set 3	Blue
I	u-e ai oa ew oi ire ear er aw ow ure are ur plain moan flew joint hire fear her paw clown pure care purse flute flur sloip graw per grear splare flowp frew stoan vuke slaig ture	Can read most B-I *real* words *without* sound blending	Review Sets 2 and 3 sounds	Grey
J	complaint holiday yesterday operate delight decide provoke pollute pronounce prepare argue surround annoy addition suspicious	Can read most B-J *real* words *without* sound blending	Child does not need *RWI Phonics* and can progress on to *RWI Spelling*	Child can progress on to *RWI Comprehension*

Move children as quickly as possible through the programme. They do not have to read each book in the set. However, there are plenty of extra books for children who need further practice.

Sound and Word Assessment 3

A	m a s d t i n p g o c k u b f e l h r j v y w v x z
B	mat leg fin rub bag men zip box kib sav med tas yop hup
C	sh th ch qu ng nk chop ship hush thin wing wink thod ving thob pash shum
D	flock still grand cliff trick glimp vill droff fump plack
E	ay ee igh ow oo oo spray feet bright blow moon cook
F	ar or air ir ou oy start horse pair twirl house boy
G	flight mouse joy fair stir star pord zair darp shay poom spow boum peeg
H	a-e i-e o-e ea shake pipe smoke clean hape gite fleap shoke
I	u-e ai oa ew oi ire ear er aw ow ure are ur brain gloat chew point fire dear her law frown pure fare nurse brute clurt sloin chaw pler grear gare glowp prew floap gume fraiz fure
J	birthday midnight survive suppose allow announce audience adventure ambition vicious horrible require

Sound and Word Assessment 3 Placement Chart

	Sound and Word Assessment	Degree of sound blending used	Speed sounds to teach and review	Ditties or Storybooks
A	No or few sounds	No blending	Teach Set 1 sounds Word Time! 1, 2, 3	
B	m a s d t i n p g o c k u b f e l h r j v y w v x z mat leg fin rub bag men zip box kib sav med tas yop hup	Needs to sound out most real and nonsense words	Review Set 1 sounds (Focus upon th, sh, ch ck) Review Word Time! 1, 2, 3 Teach Word Time! 4, 5	Ditties 1–20
C	sh th ch qu ng nk chop ship hush thin wing wink thod ving thob pash shum	Needs to sound out most real and nonsense words	Review Set 1 sounds Review Word Time! 1–5 Teach Word Time! 6, 7	Ditties 21+
D	flock still grand cliff trick glimp vill droff fump plack	Can read 6 B-D *real* words *without* sound blending	Review Set 1 sounds Review Word Time! 1–7 Teach Set 2 sounds: ay, ee, igh, ow, oo, oo	Green Purple
E	ay ee igh ow oo oo spray feet bright blow moon cook	Can read 12 B-E *real* words *without* sound blending	Review Set 2 sounds: ay, ee, igh, ow, oo, oo Teach Set 2: ar, or, air, ir, ou, oy	Pink
F	ar or air ir ou oy start horse pair twirl house boy	Can read most B-F *real* words *without* sound blending	Review Set 1 and 2 sounds Teach letter names	Orange
G	flight mouse joy fair stir star pord zair darp shay poom spow boum peeg	Can read most B-G *real* words *without* sound blending	Review Set 1 and 2 sounds Teach Set 3: a-e i-e o-e ea	Yellow
H	a-e i-e o-e ea shake pipe smoke clean hape gite fleap shoke	Can read most B-H *real* words *without* sound blending	Review Set 2 and Set 3 sounds a-e i-e o-e ea Teach rest of Set 3	Blue
I	u-e ai oa ew oi ire ear er aw ow ure are ur brain gloat chew point fire dear her law frown pure fare nurse brute clurt sloin chaw pler grear gare glowp prew floap gume fraiz fure	Can read most B-I *real* words *without* sound blending	Review Sets 2 and 3 sounds	Grey
J	birthday midnight survive suppose allow announce audience adventure ambition vicious horrible require	Can read most B-J *real* words *without* sound blending	Child does not need *RWI Phonics* and can progress on to *RWI Spelling*	Child can progress on to *RWI Comprehension*

Move children as quickly as possible through the programme. They do not have to read each book in the set. However, there are plenty of extra books for children who need further practice.

A typical route through RWI Phonics 8

The purpose of RWI Phonics is for children to complete it as quickly as possible so they will then be able to read a wide range of books that will propel their vocabulary growth.
Teach at the speed of children's decoding and not their ability to encode.
Encourage children to use the Non-fiction books and Set A Storybooks at each stage as take home books, or for extra reading practice in class if necessary.
The timings below are approximate – be guided by the attainment of the children.

Speed Sounds Set 1, blending and segmenting

	Steady pace	Fast pace
Children are taught the letter-sound correspondence for 'm' with the help of a mnemonic and how to write the grapheme 'm'	Day 1	Day 1
Children are taught more letter-sound correspondences from Speed Sounds Set 1: e.g. m, a, s, d, and t. Mnemonics are dropped once they know them well.	Week 1	Day 2
In Word Time! children are taught to blend words for reading and segment them for spelling, using the sounds they have learnt, m, a, s, d and t: e.g. mad, sad, mat.	Week 2	Days 3, 4, 5
Children are taught more Speed Sounds from Set 1 and how to blend and segment words made up of them, until they know them all at speed and can write them: m a s d t i n p g o c k u b f e l h sh r j v y w th z ch qu x ng nk	Weeks 2-6	Weeks 2, 3
Once children know the Speed Sounds Set 1 at speed and can blend, they apply their phonic knowledge to reading the Ditties: an important bridge between reading single words and stories.	Weeks 7-12	Weeks 4, 5, 6

Speed Sounds Set 2

Once children can read Ditties using sound-blending, they begin to be taught the Speed Sounds Set 2 (ay, ee, igh, ow, oo, *oo*, ar, or, air, ir, ou, oy) and apply their phonic knowledge to reading the books at Green and Purple levels and developing their writing and spelling skills through activities in the accompanying Get Writing! books.	Weeks 13-20	Weeks 7-10 Miss out Purple books
Children are taught more Speed Sounds Set 2 and apply their phonic knowledge to reading the Pink and Orange level books and the accompanying Get Writing! books.	Weeks 21-33	Weeks 10-15 Miss out Orange books 1-5

Speed Sounds Set 3

Children are taught the letter names and Speed Sounds Set 3 (ea, oi, a-e, i-e, o-e, u-e, aw, are, ur, er, ow, ai, oa, ew, ire, ear, ure) and apply their phonic knowledge to reading the books at Yellow, Blue and Grey levels and developing their writing and spelling skills through activities in the accompanying Get Writing! books.	Weeks Approx. 30	Weeks Approx. 15-20 Miss out Yellow books 1-3

Any child who falls behind the rest of the class should be supported through one-to-one tutoring as outlined on page 92 until they are back up to speed.

9 Speed Sounds lessons - Set 1

New Speed Sounds to learn	Speed Sounds to review	Ditties, Storybooks and Get Writing! books
Set 1 + blending		
	Set 1 + blending	Ditties
Set 2	Set 1 + blending	Green and Purple Storybooks and Get Writing! books
	Set 1 and 2	Pink and Orange Storybooks and Get Writing! books
From Set 3: a-e, i-e, o-e, ea (+ letter names)	Set 1 and 2	Yellow Storybooks and Get Writing! books
All of Set 3	Set 1 and 2	Blue and Grey Storybooks and Get Writing! books

Activities for one hour lesson for Y1 (P2) and above

- Speed Sounds Set 1 lessons – new and review (about 20–30 minutes)
- Word Time!: blending and segmenting (about 10 minutes)
- Build a sentence – orally, and/or Storytime (about 20 minutes)

See page 27 for organising children in the Foundation Stage.

Teaching Speed Sounds Set 1 – Introduction

Children need to be able to read the single-letter graphemes that make up most of Set 1 sounds *at speed*, and be able to blend the sounds to make words before they start the Ditties.
The lessons are taught in the order that will generate the most words to read and spell.
The children learn five sounds and then start to blend these sounds to read words and segment words into sounds to spell.

Set 1 Speed Sounds are shaded on the Speed Sounds chart on page 38.

There are a few children in every class who cannot work in a group due to poor concentration. These are the children to spot straight away so you can give them one-to-one support for five minutes on the very first day. Our aim is to avoid all later catch-up programmes! Please read one-to-one tutoring (see page 92) so you can plan this from the very start.

If some children have a different home language – and know little English – do not wait for them to speak English to start. Teach the sounds at the same time as teaching them to speak English.

If some children do not learn to blend and segment straight away, keep teaching the single letter sounds. Do not hold the children back in letter knowledge – children will continue to practise blending and segmenting every day, until they can. If, by the time the children know 26 sounds, they still cannot blend and segment independently – organise one-to-one tutoring. (See page 92.)

Simple Speed Sounds chart

Note: Set 1 Sounds are shaded on the chart below.

Consonants: *stretchy*

f	l	m	n	r	s	v	z	sh	th	ng
										nk

Consonants: *bouncy*

b	c	d	g	h	j	p	qu	t	w	x	y	ch
	k											

Vowels: *bouncy* / **Vowels:** *stretchy*

a	e	i	o	u	ay	ee	igh	ow

Vowels: *stretchy*

oo	oo	ar	or	air	ir	ou	oy

1. Sound-letter pictures are used to help the children learn the sounds quickly. Children are taught that 'm' looks like two mountains, 'a' like an apple, 's' like a snake, 'd' like a dinosaur etc.

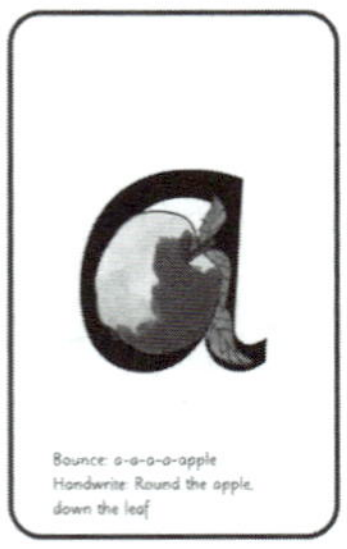

2. The sounds are either stretched or bounced – just while you teach the sound, e.g. mmmmm, sssss are stretch, d-d-d and a-a-a are bouncy
3. Some sounds are sung (voiced) and others not (unvoiced) – just while you teach the sound, e.g. mmmm, d-d-d-d, a-a-a-a are sung, sssss is not

4. Children are taught to:
   - listen to and say the sound
   - read the sound using the picture
   - write the sound using the picture-phrase

until they can read and write the sound without the support of the picture.
Make sure that children practise reading the sounds taught so far at least five times a day. Little and often is more successful that one long session.

Fred Talk

As soon as the children know a group of sounds they are introduced to a character called Fred. (Fred can be any toy, for example, a frog.)

Fred knows that there are 44 sounds in our language. He knows that sounds must be very pure and distinct so children can sound-blend.

So c-a-t = cat, ch-i-p = chip, l-igh-t = light

Try to avoid cuh-a-tuh, chuh-i-puh, luh-igh-tuh

By far the best way for teachers to become 'fluent' in Fred Talk is to do the *Read Write Inc.* training. If unfortunately this is not possible it is very important for every teacher involved in teaching *Read Write Inc.* to do the training on pages 162–169 of the *Speed Sounds Lessons Plans* handbook.

Behaviour necessary for the Speed Sounds lessons

- Children must be able to see your eyes and mouth (and you theirs), the Speed Sounds chart, your board and the Speed Sounds frieze – easily.
- Children respond to the *Stop* signal.
- Children understand and respond to the *My turn, your turn* signal.

First lesson 'm'

An example Speed Sound lesson is shown below. Detailed plans for all Set 1 Speed Sounds are in the Speed Sounds Lesson Plans handbook.

Preparation

You will need Speed Sound card 'm' – small and large 'm' Picture-Sound cards (mouse, mountain, mirror, moon) the picture frieze (at child height), the simple Speed Sounds chart, a writing board and pen.
The children will need a big writing book – plain or large spaced lined pages and a sharp pencil (and a table and chair).
Read the first lesson plan and summarise the lesson on a Post-it note.
Think of 'm' names in your class – or friends' names – or make some up!
Do not take the Handbook into the lesson – this will slow your pace.

Purpose

For children:

- To say 'm' when they read the 'm' side of the card
- To write 'm' when you say 'm'

Teaching time

- Make sure that children achieve success on the very first day - i.e. *all* the children can read and write the sound 'm'.

Hear and say m

My turn, your turn

- Sing and stretch mmmm as you press your lips together hard.
- Sing and stretch names: mmMatthew, mmMarufa, mmMolly.
- Sing and stretch, as you hold up the picture cards: mmmmmouse, mmmmirror, mmmmoon, mmmmountain (tell, don't ask what the pictures are).
- Sing and stretch, as you hold up the large Maisie and mountain card.
- Praise - a lot!

Read m

1. Copy Maisie and the mountains on the left of your board.
Run your finger down Maisie and over the two mountains, saying 'mmm'.
Say 'mountain' as you touch the end of the second mountain.

2. Write 'm' beside Maisie and the mountains - make it the same size.
Run your finger down and over 'm' saying 'mmmm'.
Say 'm' just as you touch the end of 'm'.
Repeat 1 and 2 several times.

3. Show the large Speed Sound card - picture side.
Children say 'mountain'.
Show the large Speed Sound card - letter side. Children say 'm'. Praise - a lot!
Repeat several times.

Write m

(Use '1, 2, 3 signal' to get children to tables)

My turn, your turn

1. Handwrite

Using the picture phrase Maisie, mountain, mountain air-write 'm', saying Maisie, mountain, mountain.
Do large ones in giant voices, little ones in squeaky voices.
Repeat on paper - get the children to say Maisie, mountain, mountain as they write.

2. Sound-write

Sing and stretch 'mmm', in a rhythm quietly, loudly, shouting, squeakily.
Repeat on paper - get children to say 'mmm', 'mmm', 'mmm' as they write.
Praise - a lot!

Fred Talk (oral)

Model how you say words in Fred Talk. Fred says 'm-a-n' (really emphasise the pure sounds), but we can say 'man' (really exaggerate the pronunciation so children relate 'm-a-n' to 'man')

My turn, your turn

Get the children to practise saying 'm-a-n' and 'man'.

Repeat with 'm-u-m mum', 'm-a-d mad', 'j-a-m jam'.

Praise - a lot!

Speed Sounds pack

Carry your small 'm' card around with you all day and, as you teach more, add the cards into a Speed Sound pack. Get the children to read them at every opportunity - until they can read them as easily as breathing.

Speed Sounds technique: hold the cards facing the children, do not look down - watch the children as they read, particularly your 'focus' children. If they all say the same sound - they will be right! You will only need to look down to check the card if the children hesitate. Gradually build up speed so they can all keep up.

Assessment

Check your vulnerable children:

- can say mountain when you show the picture side
- can say 'm' when you show the letter side.

If not - re-teach now.

Key teaching points

- Praise constantly: 'Mmmmarvellous'.
- Pace: be energetic and passionate in your teaching - 'I just love your "mmm"!'
- Put pencils and paper in the home corner and office areas so they can write for a purpose.
- Avoid:
  - using letter names, capital letters and joins while you are teaching Speed Sounds Set 1 and 2 lessons (see explanation, Handwriting page 91)
  - getting children to paint, roll, paste, stick letters - children don't usually say 'mmmmm' *all* the time they do these things - so it won't help at all.
  - asking children: 'What sound can you hear at the beginning of mirror, mountain etc.' 'What can you think that begins with "m"?' Tell them!

Teach all the Speed Sounds Set 1 in the same way. The lessons are all in the *Speed Sounds Lesson Plans* handbook.

- Once children know m, a, s, d, t - start blending and segmenting with these cards.

Word Time! 1: Blending and segmenting

Preparation

- Make sure you can say the sounds without the schwa (uh) e.g. 'm' not 'muh', 's' not 'suh'.
- You will need two sets of m, a, s, d and t Speed Sound cards and a pocket chart or stand to blend the words.
- The children will need magnetic boards with these letters.
- Make sure that your children can read the sounds m, a, s, d and t effortlessly.

Purpose

For children:

- to read by sound-blending: mad, sad, dad, mat, sat, Sam and nonsense words, dat, das, tas.
- to spell words through segmentation using Fred Fingers.

Teaching time

All children must believe they can read by blending the very *first* time they do it. Assist them at every stage so they achieve success, gradually removing the support until they can blend and segment independently.

Assisted blending

For each of the words mad, sad, dad, mat, sat, Sam and nonsense words, dat, das, tas:

Step 1 *Without the cards*

Say: 'You are all going to read words with these sounds today: m, a, s, d, t'

My turn, your turn

- Get the children to look at your mouth as you say the sounds in an exaggerated manner: m-a-t.
- Really feel those sounds! Repeat a few times.
- Get the children to look at your mouth as you say 'mat' in an exaggerated manner: mat.
- Really feel the sounds as you say the whole word! Repeat a few times.
- Tell the children that Fred says the word in sounds m-a-t and we say mat.
- Practise saying the word in sounds followed by the word: m-a-t, mat. Repeat a few times.

Step 2 *Blending with the cards*

Model how you:

- Say 'mat' clearly again. 'I will need "m", "a" and "t"', - place the letters in pocket chart.

My turn, your turn

- Point to the sounds and say m-a-t.
- Sweep your finger under the word and say mat - in an exaggerated manner.
- Take away the cards and repeat

Step 3 *Blending with the magnetic letters*

Model how you:

- Copy the word mat onto a child's magnetic board with the magnetic letters.
- Check the sounds are in the right order - say 'm, a, t'.
- Show how you point to the sounds with your finger and say 'm-a-t mat'. Repeat.

Step 4 *Children practise with their own magnetic letters*

- Now ask the children to find their letters m, a, t and put them on their own boards.
- Ask them to keep pointing to the sounds and reading the word until you raise your hand to stop.

Repeat with a few of the words.

Repeat every day until the children can do this quickly and easily.

Independent blending

When the children can make the words quickly in 'assisted blending', move on to help them blend independently. If this is a step too far for most children, continue assisted blending.

Model how you:

- Put out s, a, d sound cards onto your pocket chart - silently!
- Find the letters on a child's magnetic board - silently!
- Point as you say the sounds and then read the word - quietly!

Ask the children to copy you. Repeat with different words, without modelling first.

Fred Fingers

For each of the words mad, sad, dad, mat, sat, Sam and nonsense words, dat, das, tas, model how you:

- Say 'sad'
- Say the sounds as you press each sound onto three fingers: s-a-d
- Say 'sad'

Show the children how you look at your own fingers as you do this - this is what you want them to do too. Observe the children as they copy - do not join in.

Once you know children can press their fingers with the sounds:

- tell the children the number of fingers they need to get ready
- tell them the word
- ask them to press the sounds on the fingers as they say the sounds

When children can do this well ask them to write two or three of the real words. No more.

Praise - a lot!

Assessment

Make sure your most vulnerable children are sitting in your direct line of vision and observe how they manage. If you are not sure a child can blend when other children are near, assess him individually later in the day.

If you find that the entire group can blend independently, except for one or two children, organise a few one-to-ones in the afternoon until they can blend. It is vital to do this straight away. The sooner they can blend the sooner they will read.

Key teaching points

Fred Talk for reading

- Make sure you use very clear and exaggerated sounds - sloppy sounds will stop children learning to blend.
- Keep saying these words in Fred Talk through the day.
- Show the parents of children who cannot blend, at home time, how they can help at home.

Fred Fingers for spelling

- Show the children how you want them to look at their fingers, *before* you start spelling.
- Children use their non-dominant hand for fingers and the teacher must check they point in the correct reading direction.

New Speed Sounds to learn	Speed Sounds to review	Ditties, Storybooks and Get Writing! books
Set 1 + blending		
	Set 1 + blending	Ditties
Set 2	Set 1 + blending	Green and Purple Storybooks and Get Writing! books
	Set 1 and 2	Pink and Orange Storybooks and Get Writing! books
From Set 3: a-e, i-e, o-e, ea	Set 1 and 2	Yellow Storybooks and Get Writing! books
All of Set 3	Set 1 and 2	Blue and Grey Storybooks and Get Writing! books

Children begin to read the Ditties when they can read all the Set 1 sounds and can sound-blend.
It is also important to organise Storytime (see page 19) at some point during the day.

Activities for one hour lesson for Y1 (P2) and above

Speed Sounds Set 1 lessons

Spend about 10–15 minutes a day teaching and practising Speed Sounds.

- Review single letters and teach double letter sounds, ch, sh, th, ng, nk
- Word Time!: blending and segmenting

Ditty activities (35 – 40 minutes)

Spend the last ten minutes reading a 'talk about' story to the children.

Reading activities

1. Read the Speed Sounds – on the Ditty photocopy master/in the Ditty book
2. Read the Green and Red words
3. Read the Ditty
4. Re-read the Ditty and discuss the 'questions to talk about'

Writing activities

5. Build a sentence – orally
6. Hold a sentence

Children in Year 1 and above spend an hour a day, in their homogeneous group, following the activities. See page 27 for organising children in the Foundation Stage.

Introduction

The Ditties are short, simple texts with 10–20 words made up of Set 1 Sounds (Green Words) and some 'Red' Words - common words with an uncommon spelling.
The purpose of the Ditties is for children to apply the skills of sound-blending and their knowledge of Speed Sounds Set 1 to reading continuous text.
They are an important bridge between the Speed Sounds Set 1 and blending and the Storybooks.
We want the children to focus totally on decoding the words while they are at this early stage – we do not want to establish the habit of trying to guess words from pictures.
There are two different forms of Ditties – photocopiable Ditties and the Ditty books. The books are particularly helpful for children who may need extra practice.

There are 50 photocopiable Ditties, or 10 books each with five Ditties in. Most children will only need to read between 10 and 20 before being ready to move onto the Green Storybooks. Only a few children will need to read them all.

Please make sure the children move on as soon as they can read the Ditties by sound-blending the words - even if the children need to repeat the sound-blending each time they read a word.

Also available are small hardback books with Ditties in for parents to read with their children.

Behaviour necessary before reading the Ditties

Teach the children:

- To return the stop signal quickly and get their partner to do this too.
- Not to join in when you use the *My Turn* signal.
- To join in when you use the *Your Turn* signal.
- To place the Ditty between themselves and their partner.
- How to hold a pointing stick for pointing firmly.
- To sit in a good position for writing. (See handwriting position page 91.)

Activity 1: Read the Speed Sounds

Example Ditty: The shop

Speed sounds

ch sh n p o h t i r m f s a c

Green words

hot pop can shop from
chip chips

Red words

the of

hot chips from the shop
a can of pop from the shop
hot chips and pop
mmmmm

Preparation

Find the specific Speed Sound cards listed on the top of the Ditty: ch, sh, n, p, o, h, etc.

Give partners one copy of the Ditty and one pointing stick.

Make an enlarged copy of the Ditty or write it in large on the board.

Purpose

- for children to read the sounds needed for the Ditty effortlessly, particularly the double-letter sounds

Teaching time

My turn, your turn

Review the two-letter sounds in the Ditty.

- Get the children to read the Speed Sound cards – focus on two-letter sounds, sh, ch.
- Look at the children – not the cards.
- Do not join in – unless a sound needs further practice.
- Praise.

Model partner teaching

Use an enlarged photocopy of the Ditty. Model partner teaching every day until it is perfect. Ask a child to be your partner, while you take on the role as the teaching partner. Exaggerate the way you:

- **Point** underneath the sounds with your pointing stick, giving special attention to 'ch' and 'sh'. Listen carefully as your partner reads.
- **Help** your partner read every sound *correctly* – teach him the right sound if he gets stuck.
- **Praise** him when he reads the sounds well: 'Super sounds!'

Set the purpose: Ask Partner 1s to show their pointers. Say: 'Get your partner to read the sounds on the Ditty sheet in and out of order. Check your partner can read "ch" and "sh" really well. Partner 1s – point to "ch"... go!'

- Move around, praising Partner 1s.
- Use the stop signal, and then praise the teaching partners again for good pointing and helping.
- Ask Partner 1s to praise Partner 2s: 'Super sounds!'

Repeat with Partner 2s as the teacher.

Assessment

- Can *all* the children read all the single letter sounds? If not, the child should not be reading the Ditties.
- Can *all* the children read the double letter sounds? If not, place the child in your direct line of vision when you teach the group.

Key teaching points

- Can all the children see the cards easily without craning their necks?
- Are you silent when the children read the cards?

Activity 2: Read the Green and Red Words

Preparation

- Write the Green Words listed on the Ditty onto cards
- Use an enlarged copy of the Ditty
- Display the ready printed Red Words on your Red Word Wall
- Give children one copy of the Ditty and one pointing stick, between partners

Purpose

For children to practise reading the words that will be used in the Ditty

Teaching time

Green Words

My turn, your turn: read the words to the children that you predict they may have difficulty reading

(not the others). Say the word in Fred Talk - emphasising the two-letter graphemes.
Your turn: get the children to Fred Talk all the Green Words on the cards, and then read the word e.g. sh-o-p, shop; f-r-o-m, from.
Look at the children, not the cards, as they read.
Expect the children to work out the word - *do not read the word with them or to them (unless they need help).* Then, say, 'Well done you all worked the word out - yes it does say...'

Model partner teaching: use the enlarged photocopy for the first three or four Ditties while you model the partner teaching. Ask a child to be your partner.
Exaggerate the way you:

- **Point** underneath the words sound-by-sound with your pointing stick - listening carefully as your partner reads
- **Help** your partner read every word *correctly* - and say the word in Fred Talk when he gets stuck.
- **Praise** him when he reads the word successfully - 'Fabulous Fred Talk'.

Set the purpose: ask Partner 1s to show their pointers. Say: 'Get your partner to read the words on the Ditty sheet. Make sure your partner reads 'from' and 'chips' really well. Partner 1s - point to the first word... go!'

- Move around, praising Partner 1s.
- Use the stop signal, and then praise the teaching partners again for good pointing and helping.
- Ask Partner 1s to praise Partner 2s: 'Excellent words!'

Repeat with Partner 2s as the teacher.

Red Words

- Hide the Red Word to your chest.
- Tell the children the word - 'the', and say it in Fred Talk, e.g. 'th-u'.
- Repeat this a few times - 'the, th-u'
- Tell the children: 'When I show you the red card - I want you to look for the tricky letter'.
- Show the children that 'th' is 'good' but 'e' is a tricky letter because it's trying to get us to say 'e'.
- Ask the children to find 'the' in the Ditty.
- Repeat with 'of' - tricky letter 'f'.
- Display the Red Words on the Red Word Wall and practise reading these words throughout the lesson.

Assessment

- Can all the children read the simple CVC words with single sounds? If not, the child should not be reading the Ditties. The child needs more Word Time! practice with magnetic letters.
- Can all the children read CCVC and CVCC words and words with double letter sounds? If not, put extra emphasis on these words before the children read the Ditties.

Key teaching point

Do not move onto activity 3 unless you know all the children can read all the words.

Activity 3: Read the Ditty

Preparation

- Make an enlarged copy of the Ditty
- Give partners one copy of the Ditty and a pointing stick

Purpose

- For children to decode the Ditty using Fred Talk less and less on each reading

N.B. Do not read the Ditty to the children first.

Teaching time

Model partner teaching: use the enlarged photocopy while you model the partner teaching until children do it independently. Model for the top line of the Ditty - only. Ask a child to be your partner.

Exaggerate the way you:

- **Point** underneath the words, sound-by-sound with your pointing stick - listening carefully as your partner reads
- **Help** your partner read every word *correctly* - and to say the word in Fred Talk when he gets stuck.
- **Praise** him when he reads the word successfully - 'Fabulous Fred Talk'.

Set the purpose: ask Partner 1s to show their pointers. Say: 'Get your partner to read every word in the Ditty correctly. Tell your partner to use Fred Talk - if he gets stuck. Partner 1s - point to the first word... go!'

(You may want the children to read the Ditty line-by-line)

- Move around, praising Partner 1s.
- Use the stop signal, and then praise the teaching partners again for good pointing and helping.
- Ask Partner 1s to praise Partner 2s: 'Brilliant reading!'

Repeat with Partner 2s as the teacher.

Speed up the reading. Using the Ditty you have written on the board, ask the children to read the top line of the Ditty word-by-word. Praise them for having worked out the words with their partner.

Re-read the line to the children at a quicker pace and ask them to read it after you.

Repeat until they can read the whole Ditty without any Fred Talk.

Assessment

- Can the children read all the words - even if they need to use Fred Talk for every word? If not, the child needs to read easier Ditties with more CVC words.
- Can the children read some of the words without Fred Talk? If not - practise reading the words again on cards at the end of the Ditty. Praise the children when they manage to read the word without Fred Talk.
- Can the children read most or all of the words without Fred Talk on the first reading? If so - check if the child can read the later Ditties and move onto the Green books.

Key teaching point

The children will all be reading at different speeds. Get the faster readers to re-read the Ditty a few times or ask the children to read alternate lines.

Activity 4: Re-read the Ditty and discuss the 'questions to talk about'

Preparation

Have the Ditty written large on the board.

Purpose

- For children to build a mind picture from the words on the page and to read the Ditty fluently

Teaching time

- Tell the children all about your favourite *hot chips* - e.g. crispy and crunchy, fat chips, thick chips, soggy chips.
- Ask them to point to the words 'hot chips'.

Think out loud: 'When I read hot chips, I think about crispy, crunchy chips that my mum used to make.'

- Ask them to point to 'a can of pop'.
- Tell the children about your favourite pop - e.g. lemonade, fizzy orange.
- Ask children to tell their partners their favourite sort of pop.
- Model how you read the Ditty with expression, thinking about hot chips and pop.
- Ask the children to read the Ditty, chorally, as you point (do not speak).
- Ask them to take turns reading their own Ditty sheet until they can read the whole Ditty without Fred Talk.

Assessment

- Can the children answer simple questions about the Ditty? If not - help the child to speed up their reading and explain the passage again.

Key teaching point

The Ditties use words that are well within children's lexicon. If they do not understand what they are reading, it is because they are reading very slowly - or they are learning English as an additional language. Do not keep children at this stage for either of these reasons - tell them what the words mean and move on!

Activity 5: Build a sentence - orally

Purpose

- For children to build a sentence and say it out loud

Teaching time

Remind the children of your favourite *hot chips* - e.g. crispy and crunchy, fat chips, thick chips, soggy chips.

Ask: 'What are your favourite chips?' TTYP feedback: 'Popcorn' their answers.

Think out loud: 'I heard lots of you say thin crispy chips. I like crispy chips... Oh I know what we could say... *Long, thin crispy chips are the best in the world.'*

Children repeat out loud.

Ask: 'Where are you going to eat them?' TTYP feedback: 'Popcorn' answers

Think out loud: 'I heard some of you say, in the park, some said on the way home. Let me see... *Is there anything better in the world, than eating long, thin crispy chips sitting in the park?'*

Get the children to repeat the sentence, putting stress on particular words to help them say it out loud.

Assessment

Are there any children who cannot say the sentence? If so - try emphasising some of the words with greater expression and acting out the sentence. If this is still too hard - make the next sentence just a bit shorter.

Activity 6: Hold a sentence

Preparation

- The 'hold a sentence' is written at the bottom of the Ditty sheet. If you think it is too long, devise a shorter sentence.
- Give each child a notebook and pencil.

N.B. Children should not be able to see the Ditty.

Purpose

- For children to remember or 'hold' a whole sentence while focusing on spelling and spaces between each word.
- N.B. Punctuation is not taught at the Ditty stage.

Teaching time

My turn, your turn

- Say the sentence – in this example – *can I have hot chips* – and emphasise a word that will help the children remember the sentence, e.g. *can I have hot <u>chips</u>*
- Ask the children to repeat until you know they can all remember the sentence.

First word

- Ask the children to show you three fingers. (See Fred Fingers page 43.)
- Say 'can'.
- Tell them to press one sound onto each finger as they say c-a-n. (Do not join in with them or show your fingers.)
- Write the word onto the board. (Do not let a child write the word.)

Second word

- Ask the children to tell you the next word – 'I'. As this is a Red Word, write this for them.
- Say: 'I must leave a finger space before I write 'I' – otherwise the word will say canI!'
- Ask the children to read the two words in the board.

Third word

- Ask the children to tell you the next word – 'have'.
- Ask the children to show you three fingers.
- Say 'have' again.
- Tell them to press one sound onto each finger as they say h-a-v. (Do not write 'e'.)
- Say: 'I must leave a finger space before I write have'
- Write the word onto the board.
- Ask the children to read the three words on the board.

Repeat for 'hot' and 'chips'.
Ask the children to re-read the whole sentence.
Cover up or rub out the sentence.
Ask the children to pick up their pencils ready to write. Say the sentence again. Ask the children to write.

Support the children as they write – help the children write all the sounds.
If one child finishes before another, ask the quick child to write 'can I have a can of pop'.

Write the sentence on the board one word at a time and get the children to add in any letter they have missed out. Praise the children for writing each word.
Ask the children to read their own sentence again. Praise!

Assessment
Do all the children know the sounds when they put the sounds on their fingers? If not, reinforce Fred Fingers in your Speed Sounds lessons.

Key teaching points
- The children are grouped for reading progress so some children will write the sentence quickly and easily, others will write slowly.
- Support the slower writers by asking them to dictate the sounds to you.
- Give extra support to these children - often boys - in handwriting lessons later in the day (see page 91).

General points for the teaching the Ditties
- If children can't read the Ditty - they should receive more teaching of Set 1 Sounds and sound-blending. (See page 37.)
- If you have an odd number, choose three focused children to work together - and show them how to sit together.
- Sometimes, tell the children you are going to stand still and look out for excellent partner teaching.
- You may want to use the school reward system to give stickers or tokens to the teaching partners who are good at pointing/ helping/ praising.
- Don't stay with individuals.
- Practise partner teaching - pointing, helping and praising - until perfect!
- Some children keep Fred Talking even when they know the word. Model how you only use Fred Talk when you are stuck. Get the partners to tick every word that their partner does not Fred Talk.
- If a child is really struggling tell the RWI manager straight away!

Speed Sounds lessons - Set 2 11

Speed Sounds Set 2:

ay ee igh ow oo oo or ar air ir ou oy

New Speed Sounds to learn	Speed Sounds to review	Ditties, Storybooks and Get Writing! books
Set 1 + blending		
	Set 1 + blending	Ditties
Set 2	Set 1 + blending	Green and Purple Storybooks and Get Writing! books
	Set 1 and 2	Pink and Orange Storybooks and Get Writing! books
From Set 3: a-e, i-e, o-e, ea (+ letter names)	Set 1 and 2	Yellow Storybooks and Get Writing! books
All of Set 3	Set 1 and 2	Blue and Grey Storybooks and Get Writing! books

See the timetables pages 63 and 64.

Introduction

Before starting to teach Set 2 sounds, the children should be able to:

- read all Set 1 sounds effortlessly
- blend all Set 1 sounds in CVC and CCVC words
- read the Ditties independently, using sound-blending (Fred Talk) to work out new words.

Children learn Set 2 sounds while they read the Green and Purple level books, so that they will be able to move quickly through the Pink, Orange and Yellow level books.

Speed Sounds Set 2 sounds are shaded on the Speed Sounds chart on page 53.

Simple Speed Sounds chart

Note: Set 2 Sounds are shaded on the chart below.

Consonants: *stretchy*

f	l	m	n	r	s	v	z	sh	th	ng
										nk

Consonants: *bouncy*

b	c	d	g	h	j	p	qu	t	w	x	y	ch
	k											

Vowels: *bouncy* / ***Vowels:*** *stretchy*

a	e	i	o	u	ay	ee	igh	ow

Vowels: *stretchy*

oo	oo	ar	or	air	ir	ou	oy

ee

There are 12 Set 2 lesson plans in the *Speed Sounds Lesson Plans* handbook. These lessons need to be repeated until the children can read the sounds effortlessly and read the Green Words by sound-blending. Sound-phrase pictures are used to help the children learn the sounds quickly, e.g. children learn the illustrated phrase 'What can you see?' as a hook, to the learn the sound 'ee'.
Children practise reading the sounds taught so far at least five times a day. Little and often is more successful that one long session.

Behaviour necessary for the Speed Sounds lessons

- Children must be able to see your eyes and mouth (and you theirs), the Speed Sounds chart, your board and the frieze - easily.
- Children respond to the *Stop* signal.
- Children understand and respond to the *My turn, your turn* signal.

Example lesson 'ee'

An example Speed Sound lesson (from Set 2) is shown below. Detailed plans for all of Speed Sounds Set 2 are in the Speed Sounds Lesson Plans handbook.

Preparation

- You will need Speed Sound card 'ee' - small and large, the picture frieze, the simple Speed Sounds chart, a writing board and pen.
- The children will need a big writing book - large lined and a sharp pencil (and a table and chair!).
- Read the lesson plan and summarise the lesson on a Post-it note.
- Do not take the handbook into the lesson - this will slow your pace.

Purpose

For children to read and write words containing 'ee', mixed with other words.

Reading

- Listen and say the sound 'ee'
- Read the sound using the picture - 'ee, what can you see?'
- Read the sound without the picture - 'ee'
- Read the sound within mixed sounds: 't, b, j, ay, ee'
- Read the sound in words: 'tree'
- Read the sound in mixed words: 'play, tree, flat, say, back'

Writing

- Write the sound - ee
- Write the sound in words - tree
- Write the sounds in a mixed set of words: green, play, tree, flat, say, back

Teaching time

Hear and say 'ee' *(don't show the letters)*

Tell the children they are going to learn to read and spell words with the 'ee' sound.

Use *My turn, your turn*:

1. Sing and stretch 'ee'
2. Show the large picture side. Say: 'Here are two boys sitting in a tree. One says to the other... "ee, what can you see?"' (Repeat a few times.)
3. Say each of the words listed on the 'ee' picture card in Fred Talk. (Do not get the children to read these.)

Read ee

Use *My turn, your turn*. Show the card (picture side). Say: 'When we see this side of the card we say: "What can we see?"'

Show the 'ee' side. Say: 'ee'.

Explain that two letters are used to make the sound. Say 'Two letters - one sound.'

Look for the sound on the Speed Sounds poster and put the little 'ee' card in your Speed Sounds pack.

Practise reading the new card in a pack of Set 1 cards and Set 2 cards as they are taught.

Word Time!

Read with Fred Talk

Using the 'ee' Green Word cards:

- Tell the children that as they can now read the sound 'ee' they will be able to read all the words without your help.
- Hold the card to your chest - wait for all the children to get ready to read.
- Put your finger under the first sound of the word, so that when you turn it round, you can watch the slower children read the word.
- Point to the sounds as the children read in Fred Talk and then say the word. Repeat a few times.

Repeat with Set 1 Green Word cards and Set 2 cards as they are taught.

Spell with Fred fingers

Model how you:

- Show three fingers to yourself.
- Say the word: 'tree'.
- Press each finger as you say the sounds: 't-r-ee'.

For each word, e.g. 'tree'

- Say: 'Show me three' (fingers).
- Ask the children to say the word: 'tree'.
- Ask the children to press each finger as they say the sounds: 't-r-ee'.
- Say the word: 'tree'
- Ask the children to write the word: 'tree'.

Repeat with other 'ee' words and 'ay' words.

N.B. Do not show your fingers while the children show theirs.

Speed Sounds lessons - Set 3 12

Set 3 Speed Sounds is made up of alternative spellings of Set 2 sounds:
a-e ea i-e o-e u-e aw are ur er ow ai oa ew ire ear ure ti ci

New Speed Sounds to learn	Speed Sounds to review	Ditties, Storybooks and Get Writing! books
Set 1 + blending		
	Set 1 + blending	Ditties
Set 2	Set 1 + blending	Green and Purple Storybooks and Get Writing! books
	Set 1 and 2	Pink and Orange Storybooks and Get Writing! books
From Set 3: a-e, i-e, o-e, ea (+ letter names)	Set 1 and 2	Yellow Storybooks and Get Writing! books
All of Set 3	Set 1 and 2	Blue and Grey Storybooks and Get Writing! books

See the timetables pages 65 and 66.

Introduction

Before starting to teach Set 3 sounds, the children should:

- be able to read all Set 1 and 2 sounds effortlessly.
- be able to read Pink and Orange level books independently, using sound-blending (Fred Talk) to work out new words, and be reading many words, without needing Fred Talk.
- know letter names.

They will need to be able to read mixed sets of words with ea, a-e, i-e, o-e before they read the Blue level books and all the rest (above) before they read the Grey level books.

Speed Sounds Set 3 sounds are shaded on the Speed Sounds chart on page 57.

Complex Speed Sounds chart

Note: Set 3 Sounds are shaded on the chart below.

Consonants: *stretchy*

f	l	m	n	r	s	v	z	sh	th	ng
ff	ll	mm	nn	rr	ss	ve	zz	ti		nk
ph	le	mb	kn	wr	se		s	ci		
					c					
					ce					

Consonants: *bouncy*

b	c	d	g	h	j	p	qu	t	w	x	y	ch
bb	k	dd	gg		g	pp		tt	wh			tch
	ck				ge							
	ch											

Vowels

a	e	i	o	u	ay	ee	igh	ow
	ea				a-e	y	i-e	o-e
					ai	ea	ie	oa
						e	i	o

oo	**oo**	ar	or	air	ir	ou	oy	ire	ear	ure
u-e			oor	are	ur	ow	oi			
ue			ore		er					
ew			aw							
			au							

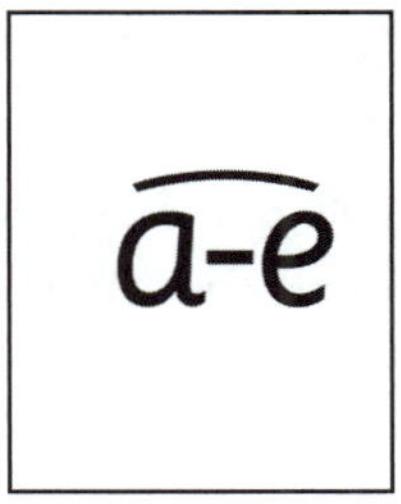

As with Set 2 sounds, sound-phrase pictures are used to help the children learn the sounds quickly, e.g. children learn the illustrated phrase 'Cup of tea?' as a hook, to learn the sound 'ee' written with the spelling 'ea'.

Children practise reading the sounds taught so far at least five times a day. Little and often is more successful that one long session.

Most of the common sounds are taught through the Set 3 lessons.

Example lesson 'ea'

Preparation

An example Speed Sounds lesson (from Set 3) is shown below. Detailed plans for all of Speed Sounds Set 3 are in the Speed Sounds Lesson Plans handbook.

- You will need speed sound card 'ea' - small and large, the picture frieze, the complex Speed Sounds poster, a writing board and pen.
- The children will need a big writing book - pages and a sharp pencil (and table and chair!)
- Read the lesson plan and summarise the lesson on a Post-it note.
- Do not take the handbook into the lesson - this will slow your pace.

Purpose

- For children to read and write words containing 'ea' mixed with other words.

Reading

- Listen and say the sound - 'ea' ('ee').
- Read the sound using the picture - ea, cup of tea?
- Read the sound without the picture - ea.
- Read the sound within mixed sounds (Set 2 + Set 3 as they are taught).
- Read the sound in words: dream, scream, etc.
- Read the sound in mixed words: (Set 2 + Set 3 as they are taught).

Writing

- Write the sound 'ea'.
- Say the sound in words - dream, scream, etc.
- Say and write the spelling in letter names.
- Write the sounds in a mixed set of words: (Set 2 + Set 3 as they are taught).

Teaching time

Hear and say 'ea' ('ee') *(don't show the letters)*

- Tell the children they are going to learn to read and spell more words with the 'ee' sound, but with a different spelling.
- Use *My turn, your turn*. Say and stretch 'eee'.
- Show the large picture side. Say: 'This child is saying "Cup of tea?"' Repeat a few times.
- Say each of the words listed on the 'ea' picture card in Fred Talk. (Do not get the children to read these.)

Read 'ea'

- Use *My turn, your turn*. Show the card (picture side). Say: 'When we see this side of the card we say: "Cup of tea?"' Show the 'ea' side. Say: 'ee'.
- Explain that two letters are used to make the sound. Say 'Two letters - one sound.'
- Look for the sound on the Speed Sounds poster and put the little 'ea' card in your Speed Sound pack. Practise reading the new card in a pack of Set 2 cards and Set 3 cards as they are taught.

Word Time!

Read with Fred Talk

Using the 'ea' Green Word cards:

- Tell the children that as they can now read the sound 'ea' they will be able to read all the words without your help.

- Hold the card to your chest - wait for all the children to get ready to read.
- Put your finger under the first sound of the word, so that when you turn it round, you can watch the slower children read the word.
- Point to the sounds as the children read in Fred Talk and say the word. Repeat a few times.

Repeat with Set 2 Green Word cards and Set 3 Green Word cards as they are taught.

Spell with Fred Fingers

Model how you:

- Say the word: 'dream'
- Show four fingers
- Press each finger as you say the sounds: 'd-r-ea-m'
- Say the word: 'dream'
- Trace the letters onto your fingers as you say the letter names: 'd-r-ea-m'
- Say the word: 'dream'

For each word, e.g. dream, ask the children to:

- Show four fingers
- Say the word: 'dream'
- Press each finger as they say the sounds: 'd-r-ea-m'
- Say the word: 'dream'
- Trace the letters onto their fingers as they say the letter names: 'd-r-ea-m'
- Say the word: 'dream'
- Write the word dream

Repeat with 'ea' and 'ee' words

Repeat with 'ea', 'ee', and a few other Set 2 words.

N.B. Do not show your fingers whilst the children show theirs.

Storybook and Get Writing! lessons 13

New Speed Sounds to learn	Speed Sounds to review	Storybooks and Get Writing! books
Set 1 + blending		
	Set 1 + blending	Ditties
Set 2	Set 1 + blending	Green and Purple Storybooks and Get Writing! books
	Set 1 and 2	Pink and Orange Storybooks and Get Writing! books
From Set 3: a-e, i-e, o-e, ea (+ letter names)	Set 1 and 2	Yellow Storybooks and Get Writing! books
All of Set 3	Set 1 and 2	Blue and Grey Storybooks and Get Writing! books

Introduction

When children can read the Ditties confidently they move onto the Green Storybooks. Children should move through the programme at the pace of their reading progress so they can complete the programme as quickly as possible.
Children must know the Speed Sounds above, before starting each set of Storybooks.

In addition to the Storybooks there are Non-fiction books and Set A Storybooks. These can be used in exactly the same way as the Storybooks following the reading activities listed. However, there are no accompanying written activities or Get Writing! books for these books. They can be used for extra reading practice of particular graphemes, should children need it, or as take home books.

Reading the Storybooks

Before children read the story they review the sounds they know and practise reading the words. The teacher introduces the story, emphasising the vocabulary they will come across in the story and the vocabulary they will use in their writing.

The children read the story three times, once to decode the words, the second time so the teacher can ensure they fully comprehend, and thirdly to discuss the story in greater depth and plan the writing they will do the next day.

The writing starts with five encoding activities, using words from the story. There are then three language comprehension activities to develop children's composition, all developed through oral drafting.

N.B. Children who have slow encoding skills are assisted throughout the programme to ensure that they are not held up by poor motor control. Children progress at the speed of their reading and not their ability to encode quickly. The aim of the programme is to finish it quickly so that children can then read books that will drive their vocabulary growth.

The blueprints for the nine reading and nine writing activities, below, are explained in greater detail on pages 67-90.

Storybook and Get Writing! lessons

The five key principles for teaching and learning are deeply embedded in all of the 18 activities.
Purpose – the teacher gets the children to repeat the purpose of the activity to their partners.
Participation – all children join in throughout the lesson with choral work using *My turn, your turn* followed by partner discussion or partner teaching.
Praise – teachers praise the teaching partners for their accurate and supportive teaching, the teaching partners praise their partner, using 'praise phrases' for performing the activity.
Pace – the lessons are dynamic and lively – there is no down time.
Passion – the more energy and exaggeration you put into your teaching, the faster the children will learn to read.

Storybook activities

There are nine reading activites:
1. Practise reading the Speed Sounds – decoding
2. Read the Green, Red and Challenge Words – decoding
3. Listen to the introduction – language comprehension
4. Discuss the vocabulary check with you – language comprehension
5. Read the story – decoding
6. Re-read the story and discuss the 'questions to talk about' – language comprehension and decoding
7. Read the story with fluency and expression – language comprehension and decoding
8. Answer the 'questions to read and answer' – language comprehension and decoding
9. Practise reading the Speed Words – decoding

N.B. Storybooks Sets 1–4 do not include activity 8.

Get Writing! activities

There are nine writing activites:
1. Play 'Fred Rhythms' to learn to spell the words – encoding
2. Play 'Fred Fingers' to memorise the spelling – encoding
3. Carry out a spelling check – encoding
4. Take a spelling test – encoding
5. Hold a sentence – encoding
6. Build a sentence – language comprehension and encoding
7. Edit for spelling and punctuation – language comprehension and encoding
8. Write a composition based on a picture strip – language comprehension and encoding
9. Write a guided composition based on a writing frame – language comprehension and encoding

N.B. Get Writing! books 1–4 only use activities 5, 7 and 8

You will need:

- A flip chart on which to write the spelling words
- A Red Word Wall – for displaying the Red Words taught so far
- A Power Words Wall – for vocabulary check words – those outside the children's spoken vocabulary
- Speed Sounds poster
- 'Thinking', 'feeling', 'happening', 'saying' bubbles

The children will need:

- Get Writing! books (one each)
- Notebooks – for spelling (one each)
- Sharp pencils
- Coloured pens

N.B. There is no need for children to write the long date or learning objective on each piece of work – save precious time by using a date stamp and asking the children to say the purpose of each activity out loud.

Behaviour necessary for the Storybook and Get Writing! lessons

Teach the children:

- To return the silent stop signal quickly and get their partner to do this too.
- To join in when you use the *Your turn* signal – while you listen.
- To sit on their chairs with feet on the floor – no heads resting on hands!
- To place the Storybook between partners.
- To sit in a good position for writing (see handwriting position page 91).

Keep practising and improving the partner teaching every day, until perfect!
Choose the best partnerships to demonstrate their behaviour in front of others.

Example timetables for Sets 1–4 of the Storybooks

Three-day plan for children making steady progress

Timetables, pages 63-66: children spend 10–15 minutes a day on Speed Sounds lessons. When children finish one book, they move straight on to the next (so if day one in this example was a Monday, they would begin a new book on the Thursday).

Day 1	Day 2	Day 3
Speed Sounds lessons: Teach Set 2 Sounds (one a day) Review Set 2 taught to date and Set 1 Sounds	Speed Sounds lessons: Teach Set 2 Sounds (one a day) Review Set 2 taught to date and Set 1 Sounds	
Reading activity 1: Practise reading the Speed Sounds p67	Reading activity 1: Practise reading the Speed Sounds p67	Reading activity 1: Practise reading the Speed Sounds p67
Reading activity 2: Read the Green and Red Words p68	Reading activity 2: Read the Green and Red Words p68	Reading activity 9: Practise reading the Speed Words p79
Reading activity 3: Listen to the story introduction p70	Reading activity 6: Read the story and discuss the 'questions to talk about' p72	Writing activity 8: Write a composition based on a picture strip p85
Reading activity 4: Discuss the vocabulary check p70	Reading activity 7: Read the story with fluency and expression p74	
Reading activity 5: ☆ Read the story p71	Writing activity 5: Hold a sentence p82	
Writing activity 5: Hold a sentence p82	Writing activity 7: Edit for spelling/punctuation p85	

The reading activities for each day lead up to the starred (☆) activity which is the main focus.

Example timetables for Sets 1-4 of the Storybooks

Two-day plan for children making speedy progress and older children

Day 1	Day 2
Speed Sounds lessons: Teach Set 2 sounds (one a day) Review Set 1 and Set 2 sounds taught to date	*Speed Sounds lessons:* Teach Set 2 sounds (one a day) Review Set 1 and Set 2 sounds taught to date
Reading activity 1: Practise reading the Speed Sounds p67 Reading activity 2: Read the Green and Red Words p68	Writing activity 5: Hold a sentence x 2 p82
Reading activity 3: Listen to the story introduction p70	Writing activity 7: Edit for spelling/punctuation p85
Reading activity 4: Discuss the vocabulary check ☆ p70	Writing activity 8: Write a composition based on a picture strip p85
Reading activity 5: Read the story ☆ p71	
Reading activity 6: Read the story and discuss the 'questions to talk about' p72	
Reading activity 7: Read the story with fluency and expression p74	
Reading activity 9: Practise reading the Speed Words p79	

The reading activities for each day lead up to the starred (☆) activity which is the main focus.

One-day plan for children receiving one-to-one tutoring

Read one book every day, and write one 'Hold a sentence'.

Example timetables for Sets 5-7 of the Storybooks

Five-day plan for children making steady progress

<table>
<tr><th>Day 1</th><th>Day 2</th><th>Day 3</th><th>Day 4</th><th>Day 5</th></tr>
<tr><td>Speed Sounds lessons: Revise Set 2, Start teaching Set 3</td><td>Speed Sounds lessons: Revise Set 2, Start teaching Set 3</td><td>Speed Sounds lessons: Revise Set 2, Start teaching Set 3</td><td></td><td></td></tr>
<tr><td>Reading activity 1: Practise reading the Speed Sounds p67</td><td>Reading activity 1: Practise reading the Speed Sounds p67</td><td>Reading activity 1: Practise reading the Speed Sounds p67</td><td>Reading activity 9: Practise reading the Speed Words p79</td><td>Reading activity 9: Practise reading the Speed Words p79</td></tr>
<tr><td>Reading activity 2: Read the Green, Red and Challenge Words p68</td><td>Reading activity 2: Read the Green, Red and Challenge Words p68</td><td>Reading activity 9: Practise reading the Speed Words p79</td><td rowspan="7">Writing activity 8: Write a composition based on a picture strip

and/or

Writing activity 9: Write a guided composition based on a writing frame

p85</td><td rowspan="7">Writing activity 8: Write a composition based on a picture strip

and/or

Writing activity 9: Write a guided composition based on a writing frame

p85</td></tr>
<tr><td>Reading activity 3: Listen to the story introduction p70</td><td>Reading activity 6: Read the story and discuss the 'questions to talk about' ☆ p72</td><td>Reading activity 7: Read the story with fluency and expression ☆ p74</td></tr>
<tr><td>Reading activity 4: Discuss the vocabulary check p70</td><td>Reading activity 8: Complete the answers to the 'read and answer' questions p78</td><td>Writing activity 4: Take a spelling test p82</td></tr>
<tr><td>Reading activity 5: Read the story ☆ p71</td><td>Writing activity 1: Play 'Fred Rhythms' p80</td><td>Writing activity 6: Build a sentence p83</td></tr>
<tr><td>Writing activity 1: Play 'Fred Rhythms' p80</td><td>Writing activity 2: Play 'Fred Fingers' p80</td><td rowspan="3">Writing activity 7: Edit for spelling/ punctuation

p85</td></tr>
<tr><td rowspan="2">Writing activity 2: Play 'Fred Fingers'

p80</td><td>Writing activity 3: Carry out a spelling check p81</td></tr>
<tr><td>Writing activity 5: Hold a sentence p82</td></tr>
</table>

The reading activities for each day lead up to the starred (☆) activity which is the main focus.

Example timetable for Sets 5-7 of the Storybooks

Three-day plan for children making speedy progress and older children

Day 1	Day 2	Day 3
Speed Sounds lessons: Revise Set 2 Start teaching Set 3	*Speed Sounds lessons:* Revise Set 2 Start teaching Set 3	
Reading activity 1: Practise reading the Speed Sounds p67	Reading activity 6: Read the story and discuss the 'questions to talk about' ☆ p72	Reading activity 9: Practise reading the Speed Words p79
Reading activity 2: Read the Green, Red and Challenge Words p68	Reading activity 7: Read the story with fluency and expression ☆ p74	Writing activity 8: Write a composition based on a picture strip or Writing activity 9: Write a guided composition based on a writing frame p85
Reading activity 3: Listen to the story introduction p70	Reading activity 8: Complete the answers to the 'read and answer' questions p78	
Reading activity 4: Discuss the vocabulary check p70	Writing activity 4: Take a spelling test p82	
Reading activity 5: Read the story ☆ p71	Writing activity 5: Hold a sentence p82	
	Writing activity 6: Build a sentence p83	
Writing activity 1: Play 'Fred Rhythms' p80	Writing activity 7: Edit for spelling/punctuation p85	
Writing activity 2: Play 'Fred Fingers' p80		
Writing activity 3: Carry out a spelling check p81		

The reading activities for each day lead up to the starred (☆) activity which is the main focus.

One-day plan for children receiving one-to-one tutoring

Read one book every one or two days and write one 'Hold a sentence'.

Storybook activities

Activity 1: Practise reading the Speed Sounds

Preparation

- Decide whether you are using the complex grapheme chart or the PowerPoint CD of page 4 of the Storybook.
- Give partners one copy of the Storybook and one pointing stick, between partners
- Note the words on page 5 (or in the story) that includes the circled graphemes.

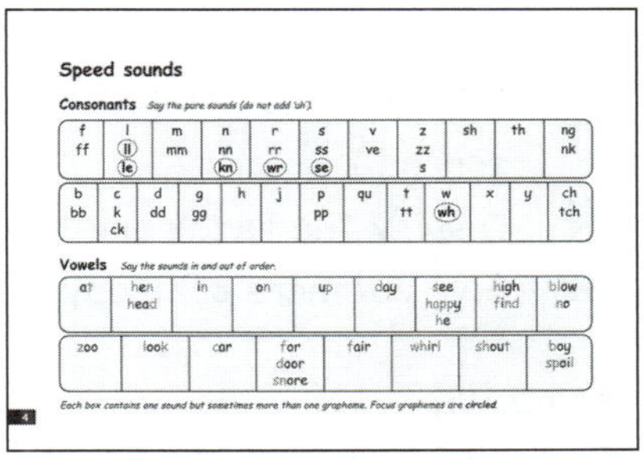
Speed sounds

Consonants *Say the pure sounds (do not add 'uh').*

f ff	l ll le	m mm	n nn kn	r rr wr	s ss se	v ve	z zz s	sh	th	ng nk		
b bb	c k ck	d dd	g gg	h	j	p pp	qu	t tt	w wh	x	y	ch tch

Vowels *Say the sounds in and out of order.*

at	hen head	in	on	up	day	see happy he	high find	blow no
zoo	look	car	for door snore	fair	whirl	shout	boy spoil	

Each box contains one sound but sometimes more than one grapheme. Focus graphemes are circled

4

Purpose

- For children to read the sounds needed for the Storybook quickly, particularly the double-letter sounds.

Teaching time

My turn, your turn: point to the circled consonant sounds on the chart and tell the children the words that they will appear in within the story e.g. 'se' in horse, 'kn' in know, 'wr' in wrap.
Ask the children to read the sounds in and out of order on the chart as you point, paying particular attention to the circled sounds and the vowels. Try to look at the children as they read. Do not join in - unless a sound needs further practice.

Model partner teaching with a child: continue to model partner teaching every day until perfect. Exaggerate the way you:

- **Point** underneath the sounds with your pointing stick, giving special attention to the sounds you want children to practise. Listen carefully as your partner reads.
- **Help** your partner read every sound *correctly* – teach him the right sound if he gets stuck.
- **Praise** him when he reads the sounds well – 'super sounds!'

Set the purpose: ask Partner 1s to show their pointers. Say: 'Get your partner to read the sounds in and out of order. Help your partner to read (specify any tricky words) really well. Partner 1s... go!'

- Move around, praising Partner 1s.
- Use the stop signal, and then praise the teaching partners for good pointing and helping.
- Ask Partner 1s to praise Partner 2s: 'super sounds!'

Repeat with Partner 2s as the teacher.

Assessment

- Observe the teaching partners. Do they make sure their partner reads the vowel sounds and the circled graphemes correctly? If not – model more!
- Can the children read the other sounds? If not – they should not be reading this book – check with the manager why the child is in your group.

Key teaching points

- Choose specific graphemes to practise when you repeat the activity on Day 2/3.
- Focus on those that children need extra practice of, particularly the vowel sounds, and the circled graphemes.
- Remember that 'pace' is one of the five Ps – this activity should last for no more than three minutes.

Activity 2: Read the Green, Red and Challenge words

Preparation

- Write onto a flip chart the Green Words that include the circled graphemes on Storybook page 4 – and any others the children need to practise. Underline the two- or three-letter graphemes. (Or use the PowerPoint CD of the words projected onto the screen.)
- Display the ready printed Red Words on your Red Word Wall
- Give partners one copy of the Storybook and one pointing stick

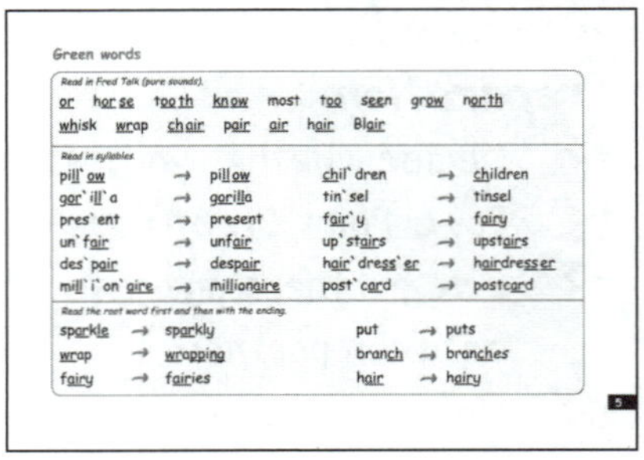

Green words

Read in Fred Talk (pure sounds).

or horse tooth know most too seen grow north
whisk wrap chair pair air hair Blair

Read in syllables

pill\`ow → pillow		chil\`dren → children	
gor\`ill\`a → gorilla		tin\`sel → tinsel	
pres\`ent → present		fair\`y → fairy	
un\`fair → unfair		up\`stairs → upstairs	
des\`pair → despair		hair\`dress\`er → hairdresser	
mill\`i\`on\`aire → millionaire		post\`card → postcard	

Read the root word first and then with the ending.

sparkle → sparkly   put → puts
wrap → wrapping   branch → branches
fairy → fairies   hair → hairy

5

Purpose

For children to practise the words that will be used in the Storybook, particularly the multi-syllabic words and any slightly tricky words.

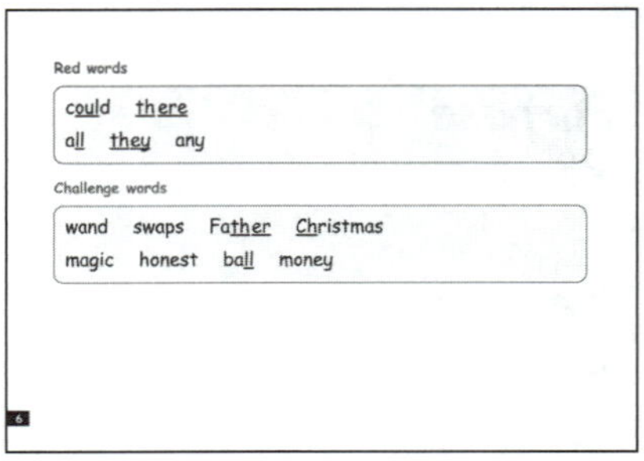

Red words

could there
all they any

Challenge words

wand swaps Father Christmas
magic honest ball money

6

Teaching time

Green Words with one syllable

(*Common words with common spellings – that have been taught)*

My turn, your turn: model how you read, in Fred Talk, the Green Words with a circled sound from the previous page.

Chorally, ask the children to read the words in Fred Talk and then the whole word.

Listen as they read – do not join in.

Model partner teaching

Exaggerate the way you:

- **Point** underneath the words sound-by-sound with your pointing stick – listening carefully as your partner reads
- **Help** your partner read every word *correctly* – and say the word in Fred Talk if he gets stuck.
- **Praise** him when he reads the word successfully – 'Fabulous Fred Talk/Excellent word reading'.

Set the purpose: ask Partner 1s to show their pointers. Say: 'Get your partner to read the first set of words on page 5. Make sure your partner reads (specify any tricky words) really well. Partner 1s – point to the first word... go!'

- Move around, praising Partner 1s.
- Use the stop signal, and then praise the teaching partners again for being such good pointers and teachers.
- Ask Partner 1s to praise Partner 2 - 'Super sounds!' 'Excellent words!'

Repeat with Partner 2s as the teacher.

Green Words with two or three syllables

My turn, your turn

1. Read each syllable in Fred Talk and then as a complete exaggerated syllable – e.g. *d-e-s, des; p-er, per, ay-t, ate.*
2. Read the whole word in exaggerated syllables: *des- per -ate.*
3. Read the whole word: desperate.

Ask the children to read the words, chorally.

Listen as they read – do not join in.

Green Words: roots and endings

My turn, your turn

1. Read the root and then the whole word, exaggerating the ending.
2. Ask the children to read the words, chorally.

Listen as they read, do not join in.

Model partner teaching

Exaggerate the way you:

- **Point** underneath the words syllable-by-syllable with your pointing stick – listening carefully as your partner reads
- **Help** your partner read every word *correctly* – and say each syllable in Fred Talk if he gets stuck.
- **Praise** him when he reads the word successfully – 'Super syllables'.

Set the purpose: ask Partner 1s to show their pointers. Say: 'Get your partner to read the words on page 5. Make sure your partner reads (specify any tricky words) really well. Partner 1s – point to the first word... go!'

- Move around, praising Partner 1s.
- Use the stop signal, and then praise the teaching partners again for good pointing and helping.
- Ask Partner 1s to praise Partner 2s: 'Excellent words!'

Repeat with Partner 2s as the teacher.

Red Words

(Common words with uncommon spellings)

My turn, your turn

- Teach any new Red Words in the story.
- Hide the Red Word to your chest e.g. 'could'.
- Tell the children the word – 'could', and say it in Fred Talk e.g. 'c-*oo*-d'.
- Repeat this a few times – could – c-*oo*-d
- Tell the children: 'When I show you the red card – I want you to look for the tricky letter/s.'
- Show the children that 'c' and 'd' are 'good' but 'o' and 'u' and 'l' are tricky letters.

Display the Red Words on the Red Word Wall.

Ask the children to read these words as you point to the words in and out of order.

Change the position of the Red Words regularly.

Challenge Words

(Content words necessary to the story)

My turn, your turn: challenge the children to read the words, but help immediately if they are *too* challenging.

Assessment

- Observe the teaching partners.
- Do the teaching partners make sure their partners read all the Green Words, including the multi-syllable ones, correctly? If not – repeat the teaching of those they find difficult.
- Can they read the Red Words without hesitation? If not – practise reading the Red Words throughout the day – and when back in the class. If some children have not been taught as many words as others, the practice will help for future books.

Key teaching points

- Make a note of any words children find difficult and practise again.
- The more energy and emphasis you put into teaching the words the more likely it is that the words will be stored in the children's orthographic store.

Activity 3: Listen to the introduction

Preparation

- Read the story and prepare your introduction to the story before the lesson so you can 'sell' the story to the children – as though you were planning the blurb on the back of a book.

Hairy fairy

Introduction

Would it be fair if you kept losing your job before you knew if you were any good at it or not? Is it right to have to change yourself just to fit in with other people?

This story is about a fairy.
He has a beautiful dress, a wand and wings just like other fairies but… there's a problem. He is covered in thick hair. Imagine what problems that gives him. No one will give him a job. But in the end he finds the perfect solution and he ends up better off than all the other fairies.

Find out how.

Story written by Gill Munton
Illustrated by Tim Archbold

7

Purpose

- For children to have a general overview of the story and to understand the meanings of unfamiliar words or phrases.

The teacher needs to inspire children to want to read story:

- to activate prior knowledge
- to introduce and teach the core ideas and vocabulary necessary to the story (including vocabulary check words)
- to emphasise new second and third layer vocabulary and phrases that you want to use in the children's writing

Teaching time

Partner discussion: make your introduction last about three minutes. Ask the children to turn to their partners to answer questions and only take quick feedback. Above all, make it lively!

Example:

'This story is all about a fairy. This is an unusual fairy. Most fairies are dainty and… (TTYP and 'Popcorn'.) Yes, pretty, delicate, floaty. Pink.

Not this one. He looks coarse and hairy. The fairy queen has quite a task on her hands trying to find him a job.

Oh the *sense of anticipation and excitement* he feels when he goes to his new job! But then what *despair* he feels when he gets the sack – when the fairy says he has to go. The *humilation! The desperation!* Poor hairy fairy.

Let's read the book to find out if he gets a job. Thumbs-up for yes. Thumbs-down for no.'

Key teaching points

- Do not read the story introduction on page 7 as a script – use your own ideas.
- Keep to the point and use *quick* feedback ('Choose two', 'Paraphrase', 'Popcorn' or a choral response).
- Think about the writing you will be modelling – the introduction is a good time to start feeding in ideas.
- Avoid selecting children who raise their hands to answer.

Activity 4: Discuss the vocabulary check

Preparation

- Read through the story to select further vocabulary and phrases that may need to be explained to your children – in the context of the story, either adding in words/phrases or concepts or leaving out the more common ones.
- Add the words on cards onto your Power Word Wall – not the definition.

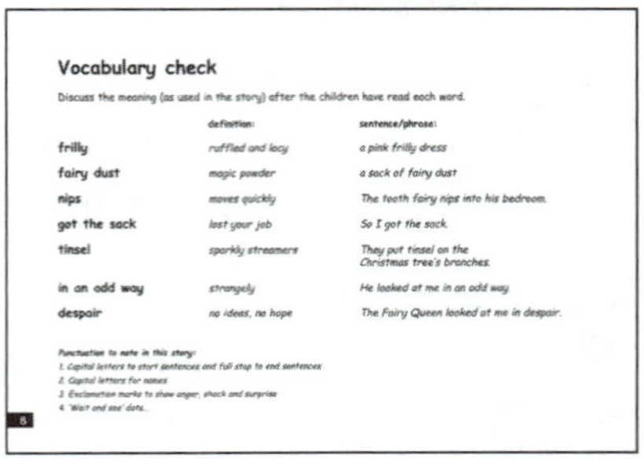

Vocabulary check

Discuss the meaning (as used in the story) after the children have read each word.

	definition:	sentence/phrase:
frilly	*ruffled and lacy*	*a pink frilly dress*
fairy dust	*magic powder*	*a sack of fairy dust*
nips	*moves quickly*	*The tooth fairy nips into his bedroom.*
got the sack	*lost your job*	*So I got the sack.*
tinsel	*sparkly streamers*	*They put tinsel on the Christmas tree's branches.*
in an odd way	*strongely*	*He looked at me in an odd way.*
despair	*no ideas, no hope*	*The Fairy Queen looked at me in despair.*

Punctuation to note in this story:
1. Capital letters to start sentences and full stop to end sentences
2. Capital letters for names
3. Exclamation marks to show anger, shock and surprise
4. 'Wait and see' dots…

8

- Identify second and third layer words (see page 16) in the vocabulary check. These are the words you will continue to display after the children have finished reading the story.
- Display illustrations – if appropriate.

Purpose

- For children to learn new vocabulary needed to understand the text

Teaching time

My turn, your turn: touch each word on the Power Word Wall as you say it.
Ask the children to repeat the word.

- Give a brief definition of the word – just as it is used in story.
- Use quick and simple drama to give emphasis to second layer words e.g. nips – use your finger to show how the fairy nips in and out of rooms.
- Touch the word as you say it. The children must hear, see and repeat the word in your teaching and conversation throughout the day.

Assessment

- Do the children use some of these words in their own writing?
- If not – model how you use the words explicitly when you introduce the writing activity.

Key teaching points

- Give vivid explanations – do not ask, 'Who can tell me the meaning of...?' TELL!
- On subsequent days, once you are sure that children know the meaning, ask them to turn to their partners to say the meaning of each word.
- Use the second and third layer words throughout the lessons.

Activity 5: Read the story

- The children are now ready to read the text for themselves: they have practised reading the sounds and words and you have motivated them to want to read the story.
- Don't read the story to the children first; emphasis on the first reading is upon decoding, so they need the chance to do this.
- Don't ask for, or expect, expression; if children do read with insightful intonation on the first reading the text is too easy.

Preparation

Read the story thoroughly yourself before the lesson – predict the words you will need to help the children read.

Purpose

- For children to read the text independently and to help their partner read every word correctly – no guessing!

Teaching time

Model partner teaching: model the partner teaching for the first few lines on page 9. Ask a child to be your partner.

Hairy fairy

I'm a fairy. I am - honest!
I've got all the right things.
I've got a pink frilly dress ...
a pair of sparkly boots ...
a sack of fairy dust ...
a pair of gold wings ...
and a magic wand to whisk in the air.

But - and it's a big but - I'm hairy! Very hairy indeed.

9

Exaggerate the way you:

- **Point** underneath the words, sound-by-sound with your pointing stick – listening carefully as your partner reads.
- **Help** your partner read every word *correctly* – and say the word in Fred Talk if he gets stuck.
- **Praise** him when he reads the word successfully – 'fabulous Fred Talk!'

Set the purpose: ask Partner 1s to show their pointers. Say: 'Get your partners to read every word on the page correctly. Tell your partners to use Fred Talk – only if they get stuck. Partner 1s – point to the first word... go!'

Partners swap roles at the bottom of each page.
Tell the children that, if *both partners* cannot read a word, they should alert you by *both partners* putting their hands on their heads.

- Move around, praising the teaching partners.
- Use the stop signal, and then praise the teaching partners again for good pointing and helping.
- Ask partners to praise each other's reading – 'good reading!'.

Speed up the children's reading

- Some children will have read the story slowly. In order to give the children a full sense of the story read the story aloud to them.
- Ask Partner 1s to use the pointing stick to point under each word as you read aloud.
- Ask Partner 2s to check that their partners track well.
- Ask both partners to jump in when you hesitate. This keeps both partners on task.

Assessment

- Observe the teaching partners.
- Do they make sure their partners use Fred Talk to read unfamiliar words? Do they make sure their partner reads all the Green Words, including the multi-syllables correctly? If not – strengthen your teaching of Green Words before you ask children to read the text. You must *know* that children can read the words *before* they read the story.

Key teaching points

- The teacher's role is monitoring the whole group – do not stay with individuals.
- Constantly notice and praise successful partner teaching.
- Ask partners to read alternate pages and then go back to the beginning if they finish.
- If any children are struggling – ***tell the RWI manager then and there!***
- Avoid 'round robin' reading – you will lose full participation.
- Only use choral reading when you want the children to copy how you read a sentence.
- When children can read the Blue and Grey books quickly, let them track their partner's reading in their own copy of the book.

Activity 6: Read the story and discuss the 'questions to talk about'

Preparation

- Plan your 'think out louds' for each page – to explain and clarify children's understanding of the story.
- Plan your 'Find it' and 'Prove it' questions to follow your explanation of the story.

Purpose

- For children to understand the story – every word, paragraph and page!

Teaching time

Explain and clarify the story to the children to ensure they engage clearly with the text.

- *Think out loud* how you check your own understanding of the story.
- Ask the children to track the text as you read each passage to the children, *thinking out loud*, so the children 'see' what you think. Tell them that you are letting them see inside your mind as you read – as if you have a thinking bubble coming out of your head.
- Don't make it look too easy! Hesitate as you *think out loud*. Ask *yourself* questions and answer them *yourself*. Always give your reasons; explain why.
- *Think out loud*: 'I wonder if… Let me check this… What's all this about then…? Aaaaah… I think he's saying this because… I bet he's feeling really… now that… I can see what's going to happen now… So in this story, this words means…'
- Exaggerate the *think out loud* to engage children in the story – it is *planned* chatter!
- Bring the children into the *think out loud* – ask them to find the words and phrases you are talking about.

Questions to talk about

Once you think the children understand each page ask the children your 'Find it' and 'Prove it' questions.

'Find it' questions – simple questions that are right there 'on the page' e.g. *What is happening?*

'Prove it' questions – more involved questions that ask the children to empathise or use evidence, e.g. *You are* (supply character): *how do you feel? What are you thinking? What are you going to do…? What would you say if…?*

Ask the children to turn to their partners to discuss every question. Watch and listen to the children as they talk.

Feed back using 'Choose Two', 'Paraphrase', 'Popcorn' or 'Choral'.

Re-read the story

When you have finished discussing the story, ask the children to re-read the story. You may want to do this page-by-page or get them to re-read the story at the end.

Assessment

- Observe the teaching partners as they listen to their partner read the text.
- Do they make sure their partners read the text with minimal Fred Talk? If not – make a note of the words they are having difficulty with and review.
- Do they encourage their partner to use meaningful intonation? If not, you may need to strengthen your explanation of the text extend your *thinking out loud.*
- Can you point to any word in the text and both partners know its meaning? If not – go through your vocabulary check every day – provide illustrations/ act out the word. Check if there are other words that need to go on the Power Words Wall.

Key teaching points

- This activity should *teach* comprehension – not *test.*
- Use your own questions – the ones provided are default ones for supply teachers and short notice lessons.

- Do not hold children back because they appear not to understand the story – tell them what it is about!
- Don't get too involved with one partnership when they are talking – check that the whole class are talking
- Do not choose children to talk who raise their hands to feed back

Activity 7: Read the story with fluency and expression

The greater the children's understanding of the vocabulary, characters' feelings, thoughts and motivation the more likely they are to read with appropriate intonation and expression.
We use three activities to help build the bridge between the reading and the writing: bubbles, punctuation mimes and power words.

1. Using the bubbles

Preparation

On your Power Word Wall make a pocket for each of the five of the basic emotions, saying and moving words.
Label each pocket: e.g. happy, surprised, angry, sad, frightened (first layer words).

Behind each word, start to collect second layer words as you use them, through this lesson and other lessons through the day, e.g:

'Feeling' words
happy: cheerful, jolly, glad, elated, ecstatic, joyful, optimistic
surprised: amazed, astonished, shocked
angry: irritated, annoyed, grouchy, grumpy, frustrated, exasperated, full of loathing, full of resentment, full of disgust
sad: hurt, anguished, depressed, desperate, hopeless, gloomy, glum, unhappy, sorrowful, miserable, melancholy, lonely, rejected, homesick, dejected, insecure, embarrassed, humiliated, insulted, pessimistic
frightened: alarmed, shocked, horror-struck, terrified, panic-stricken, hysterical, mortified, anxious, nervous, tense, uneasy, apprehensive, worried, distressed, full of dread

'Saying' words
say: utter, announce, answer, reply, suggest
shout: yell, roar, bellow, shriek, scream, call, cry, rant
whisper: murmur, mumble, hiss, sigh
whine: grumble, grouch, complain

'Moving' words
Walk: stroll, saunter, amble, trudge, plod, dawdle, hike, tramp, tromp, slog, stomp, trek, march, stride, roam, traipse
Run: sprint, race, dart, rush, dash, hurry, scurry, scamper, bolt, fly, gallop, charge, shoot, hurtle, speed, zoom, go like lightning, go like the wind
Creep: steal, sneak, slip, slink, sidle, pad, edge

Purpose

- For children to use new vocabulary in discussion (second and third layer words) and to consider the motivation of characters – *What are they feeling or thinking? What could they be saying?*

This activity will help you to model how we infer meaning, beyond the words on the page and to build links between the reading and writing process

Teaching time

- Explain to the children that they are going to read the story again, and you have chosen three pages that you will discuss in greater depth.
- For the pages you have not chosen to talk about, read the page to the children with appropriate expression.
- For the three pages you have chosen to talk about using the bubbles, follow the guide for each bubble below.

'Feeling' bubble – *for pages where characters are experiencing one of the key emotions*
Give children the possible options for how a character is feeling.
E.g. 'I wonder how the fairy is feeling? Is he feeling *excited* about being a fairy, or does he feel *worried* that he is a fairy?' (Touch the two cards on your pocket chart.)
TTYP and choral response: thumbs up, say: 'excited', thumbs down, say: 'worried'.
Ask them why. TTYP and 'Choose Two', e.g. 'Because he's got a new job'.
Build on/clarify what the children say, e.g.
'Ashraf thinks he's excited about his future because he's got a new job.'
Ask the children to repeat.
Ask the children to read the paragraph/page showing how the fairy feels.
In later texts, once children have been taught many second layer 'feeling' words, ask them to decide how they think the characters are feeling and how they will read the passage.

'Saying' bubble – *for pages where there is little or no speech on the page*
Use the 'saying' words on your Power Word Wall.
Discuss what a particular character is saying and then how he or she is saying it.
Put the children in role as a character in the story, e.g.
Say: 'We are all Mrs Blair complaining to Mr Blair – we really don't like the fairy do we? I'll start:
"So then dear, what do you think of our new fairy then?"
"I think it's awful. Its hairy and ugly and..."'
Ask the children to TTYP. Feed back using 'Choose Two': He's horrid/ He looks silly.
Build upon what the children say: 'Absolutely. Not only is he ugly and horrid, he's wearing a silly dress too!'
Get the children to repeat.
Ask 'What do we want to do?' TTYP and paraphrase feedback:
'So shall we send him back? Shall we complain? What shall we say?'
And so on...

Discuss how the character is talking by giving children options. *Think out loud:* 'I wonder whether Mrs Blair is sighing or grumbling, or maybe she is bellowing?'
We've added a bit more to the story here. Ask the children to re-read the page, and stop at the point when Mrs Blair moans.

***'Thinking' bubble** – for a page where a character is feeling particularly happy, sad, angry, surprised or frightened.*
Think out loud as you take on the role of a particular character. Show how the characters may be saying one thing but thinking something else, e.g.
'I am the hairdresser. I am astonished!' (touch the Power Words Wall) 'I have never, in my whole life, ever seen a fairy so hairy. I have had to work all day to cut it all off.'
Ask the children to TTYP and say what the fairy may be thinking.
Feed back using 'Choose two' or 'Paraphrase'.
Build upon the children's ideas as for the saying bubble.

***'Happening' bubble** - for a page where you could explain the action in greater detail*
Think out loud what could be going to happen next, or give further explanation for what is going on, e.g. 'I wonder what the fairy will do for the rest of the year... maybe he'll go somewhere hot and luxurious now that he is a millionaire. Maybe he'll...'
TTYP. Feed back using 'Choose two' or 'Paraphrase', e.g. 'He'll never work again. He'll go somewhere nice. He'll use his money to look more beautiful.'
Think out loud: 'Let me try out some of those ideas... After wrapping his last present of the year, the hairy fairy decided enough was enough – no more present wrapping. No more work. He put on a lovely new coat, said a big thank you to Father Christmas, and went on his way.'
Ask children to TTYP, to try putting their own new ending to the story.
Give the children the stem you want them to start with: 'After wrapping his last present of the year...'

Ask the children to read the whole book again, taking turns, partner by partner.

2. Punctuation mimes

Preparation

Choose the punctuation from the story that you plan to use in the 'picture strip' writing the next day. Choose one or two pages to model how the punctuation affects the way we read.

Purpose

- For children to increase fluency and accuracy of reading and to learn how the author uses punctuation to give further meaning to the text.

Teaching time

Think out loud as you deliberate how the punctuation helps you understand the passage, e.g.
'There's an exclamation mark coming up – I wonder if the fairy is feeling very excited or is he very worried? I'd better read that again – I didn't make the fairy sound full of despair. Whoops! I forgot to read that comma – it's there to let me know this is a pause. Do you think my voice told you there was a question then?'

Ask the children to mime the actions as you read. Slow down and exaggerate your reading so children can *feel* the punctuation and join in more easily.
Introduce the punctuation mimes (below) one-by-one, story-by-story.
Partner work: Ask partners to read alternate sentences – using the punctuation as they read. Or ask Partner 1 to read as Partner 2 mimes the punctuation.

Punctuation mimes

- *Full stops*
  Exaggerate how your voice drops at the end of a sentence.
  Mime action: punch the air
- *Capital letters* (for use in the writing lessons)
  Put your hands together and bow briefly.
- *Exclamation marks*
  Exaggerate the particular feeling in the sentence.
  Mime action: downward stroke as you say – '*wiiiith*'
  Punch as you say *'feeling'*
  Ask the children: 'Did you hear my excitement/ astonishment/ conviction/ surprise…?'
  Model how you have to scan quickly to the end of a sentence to spot punctuation ahead.
- *Question marks*
  Exaggerate the raise in pitch of your voice.
  Mime action: raise eyebrows as you draw a question mark in the air.
  Model how you have to scan quickly to the end of a sentence to spot punctuation ahead.
- *Commas*
  Mime action: twist a wrist
- *Speech marks*
  Mime action: open speech marks with two fingers of their left hand and close the speech marks with two fingers of the right.
- *Ellipsis*
  Exaggerate the time you 'wait and see'
  Mime – three short pokes with a forefinger

Practise reading the page chorally – only when children have learnt the punctuation and discussed how it affects the meaning of the passage.

3. Power words

Preparation

Select two pages that include sentences with a power word – a special word that helps us build a strong mind picture, e.g. *The fairy creeps upstairs and nips into his bedroom.*

Purpose

- For children to collect strong vocabulary for writing

Teaching time

Think out loud why you have chosen these as power words, e.g. 'I like "creeps" – it shows me how the fairy moves. I can see the fairy *creeping* upstairs' (use your fingers to creep) 'and then "nipping" into his bedroom' (use fingers to move quickly).

The author could have written:
The tooth fairy went upstairs, and went into the bedroom – but there are no power words!

Use the power words wall to collect some more words that have a similar meaning to creep: sneak, slip, slink, sidle, pad, edge.

'Let's get the fairy to sneak and slip – use your fingers.
How are you moving?'
TTYP. Feed back using 'Popcorn', e.g. quietly, carefully.
'Careful of the squeaky floor boards! Lift your feet so you doesn't make a noise.'

Key teaching point
Add these words on your Power Words Wall to use the next day when they write their story strip.

Assessment
Can the children read the text with appropriate expression?
Are children using the bubbles, punctuation and power words in their picture strip writing? If not, focus on one of the above more thoroughly. Choose just one or two pictures next time.

Activity 8: Answer the 'questions to read and answer'

Activity 8 only appears in Sets 4–7 of the Storybooks and Non-fiction books.

Purpose

- For children to show their understanding of the text and to practise answering 'comprehension questions'

Teaching time

The 'questions to read and answer' are written in words that the children can decode. They require the children to choose the correct answer, complete a sentence or write a full answer.

Questions to read and answer
(Children complete without your help.)

1. The fairy had a **red spotty dress / a short black dress / a pink frilly dress.**
2. The tooth fairy swapped the tooth for **some sweets / money / a storybook.**
3. Mrs Blair said that a hairy fairy looked **fantastic / all wrong / very silly.**
4. The Fairy Queen sent him to **the hairdresser / the shops / the zoo.**
5. The hairy fairy is **very poor / very rich / very unhappy** at the end.

Model how to *think out loud* how to work out the answers by searching back in the text. Then answer the question carefully, e.g. 'I can see straight away what the answer is, but I am going to read all of the answers carefully to make sure there isn't a better answer. I'm going to see how quickly I can check the answer and write the page number in my notebook.'

Partner work: ask Partner 1 to answer the first question, orally, and for Partner 2 to support. Swap roles after each question.

Decide whether you want the children to write the answer down, give a choral response, or place their finger on the evidence.

Assessment
Can the children read the questions independently and find the answers quickly? If not – check they can read the story. If yes, give extra support to find the answers. Observe the partners.

Key teaching point

Make this pacey – do not let children spend long writing their answers – this is a reading activity.

Activity 9: Practise reading the Speed Words

Preparation

Write on the board the words from the story that the children have had the most trouble reading

Speed words *Children practise reading the words across the rows, down the columns and in and out of order clearly and quickly.*

children	before	tooth	horse	sparkly
too	hairy	fairy	upstairs	pair
unfair	chair	could	anything	most
don't	so	they	ball	very

18

Purpose

- For children to build reading speed – to increase the number of words in their orthographic store.

Teaching time

My turn, your turn: as you point, say the harder words very clearly. Ask the children to read the words, chorally, in and out of order. Listen as they read – do not join in.

Model partner teaching

Exaggerate the way you:

- **Point** underneath the words with your pointing stick – listening carefully as your partner reads
- **Help** your partner read every word *correctly* – and say each word/syllable in Fred Talk when he gets stuck. If your partner hesitates or makes an error, ask him to start again at the beginning of the row
- **Praise** him when he reads the word successfully.

Set the purpose: ask Partner 1s to show their pointers. Say: 'Get your partner to read across the rows, down the columns and then in and out of order. Partner 1s – point to the first word... go!'

- Move around, praising Partner 1s.
- Use the stop signal, and then praise the teaching partners again for good pointing and helping.
- Ask Partner 1s to praise Partner 2s: 'Speedy reading!'

Repeat with Partner 2s as the teacher.

Assessment

Can all the children read the words, only using Fred Talk to read a few harder words? If not, keep a keen eye on your most vulnerable readers. If they need to Fred Talk every word, they are likely to need a lot more practise at this level of Storybooks. Or you may have gone too quickly through the decoding activities.

The nine writing activities

Activity 1: Play 'Fred Rhythms' to learn to spell the words

Preparation

Copy the Green and Red Words onto your flipchart from the spelling section in the Get Writing! book. Add any common words that children have had difficulty spelling with from their last piece of writing in the children's 'Your Words' box.

Purpose

- For children to identify any potential problem grapheme in the word

Teaching time

For each Green and Red Word listed in the section:
Think out loud as you look at the word and consider if there is a problem grapheme.
Example word – horse
'I think the "se" in horse may cause us a problem – let's say this – with attitude!' (Use letter names)
Look at the Speed Sounds chart and point to 'se' in the sound box.
Say 'se' – the alternative grapheme for 's' with attitude.
(If there is no problem – don't invent one.)

For each Green and Red Word listed in the section:
My turn
Read the word: horse.
Read the sounds in Fred Talk: 'h- or- se'.
Say the word again.
Now say the spelling (letter names) in a rhythm – se – with extra attitude: 'h – or – **se**'
Say the word again.
Your turn
Get the children to repeat as you point to the graphemes – do not join in.
Repeat with all the Green and Red Words.
Use a 'nasty' voice for the difficult grapheme in the Red Word, as that is the part of the word that is the hardest.

Key teaching point

There is often a direct correlation between children's success in spelling the words and the teacher's energy and enthusiasm. The greater the attitude the greater the success.

Assessment

Observe the children as they say the sounds and graphemes (do not join in) – make sure your vulnerable children are joining in.

Activity 2: Play 'Fred Fingers' to memorise the spelling

Preparation

Make sure that children cannot see the words you are about to spell.

Purpose

- For children to practise saying the sounds and spelling – remembering the grapheme with attitude (without looking at the word)

Teaching time

Before you start, make sure your children know how to hold and touch their Fred Fingers (see page 59).
Example word: horse
My Turn
For each Green and Red Word listed in the section:
Say: (example) 'I need three fingers.'
Say 'horse'.
Say the sounds as you press each sound onto three fingers – 'h-or-se.'
Say 'horse'.
Say the spelling (letter names) as you trace the graphemes onto three fingers – putting attitude onto 'se'
Say 'horse'.

Speed up when you are sure the children can put the rhythm onto their fingers.

Key teaching points

- This is the same as the Fred Fingers activity in the Word Time! lesson.
- Show the children how you want them to look at their fingers, before you start spelling.
- Children use their non-dominant hand for fingers and the teacher must check they point in the correct reading direction.
- Talk is the key. By being able to articulate the possible errors they will make, the children will be less likely to make them.

Assessment

Do all children exaggerate the problem grapheme? If not, re-model.

Activity 3: Carry out a spelling check

Preparation

Children need a jotter and a sharp pencil

Purpose

- For children to practise spelling words with the tricky grapheme.

Teaching time

Model partner teaching
Exaggerate the way you:

- **Help** your partner identify the tricky grapheme – say the problem grapheme out loud with attitude.
- **Spell** every word *correctly* – saying the sounds and spelling if he gets stuck.

Set the purpose: tell Partner 1s that they are the teacher. Say: 'Get your partner to spell the Red Words first and then the trickier Green Words. For example, make sure your partner spells "could" with "oul".'

- Move around, praising Partner 1s.
- Use the stop signal, and then praise the teaching partners again for helping their partner spell the words.
- Ask Partner 1s to praise Partner 2s: 'Great spelling!'

Repeat with Partner 2s as the teacher.

Key teaching point

Praise the teaching partners who help their partners practise the tricky part of the word.

Assessment

Observe the children as they support their partner. Does the teaching partner help their partner learn the trickier part of the word? Can the children spell the trickier words? If yes, move onto activity 4. If not, keep playing 'Fred Rhythms' and 'Fred Fingers"

Activity 4: Take a spelling test

Preparation

You will need a pen and board; children will need their spelling jotters, a pencil and a coloured pen

Purpose

- For children to check they can spell the words

Teaching time

Say the words from the spelling list. Ask the children to write them down.
Ask children to mark their own spellings with a coloured pen:
Write the word on the board e.g. 'horse'.
Say: 'If you wrote "se" in "horse", give it a tick. If not – change it.'
Repeat with the other words
Praise the children for correcting the words.

Key teaching points

- Be generous with ticks.
- Build an atmosphere where children feel safe and happy to share their errors with the class.
- Continue to display the harder words

Assessment

Are the children using the correct spelling in their own writing? If not, repeat the teaching of the harder words the following week.

Activity 5: Hold a sentence (see sentences at the back of the Get Writing! books)

Preparation

- If the sentences chosen are too hard or too easy, change them.
- You will need a board and a pen; the children will need their Get Writing! books, a pencil and a coloured pen.

Purpose

- For children to develop the ability to 'hold' a total sentence before writing
- For children to practise encoding and secretarial skills

Teaching time

My turn, your turn

Say the sentence and ask the children to repeat.

Repeat using different voices, emphasising the same words each time until the children can say the sentence clearly.

Add the punctuation mimes (see page 77).

Ask the children to open their books, pick up their pencil and repeat the sentence again.

Support the children as they write.

Write the sentence word by word on the board.

Ask the children to mark their own sentence with a coloured pen.

Reinforce learning by giving the children lots of ticks for remembering punctuation and the trickier graphemes.

Key teaching point

Do not underestimate the number of times you need to repeat the sentence before children can 'hold' it. You may need to do this five or six times.

Assessment

Make a note of common errors so you can add these to the 'Your words' section in the Get Writing! books.

Activity 6: Build a sentence

The children will have had plenty of practise in building sentences out loud since the beginning of the programme. They will now start to write the sentence that they have built with you.

However, some children encode quickly and so remember their sentence, while others encode slowly and need support in remembering the sentence.

In a few instances, you will need to ask the child to write the first few words and dictate the rest to you.

The more we help the children become quick encoders the sooner they will be able to remember to 'hold' the thought while they write. Handwriting lessons, at a different time of the day, will help children speed up their writing (see page 91).

We must know, before the children pick up their pencils, that *they* know what they will write – that they can hold their sentence out loud.

Preparation

- Decide if you want to change the word provided. You may want to choose a synonymous word.
- Decide whether you want the children to write a group sentence or do paired or individual writing.
- Display the sentences and words. This work must feed into children's creative writing – make explicit links for children.

Purpose

- For children to build a picture that includes and shows the meaning of a given word

Teaching time

Example word: *despair* from The Hairy Fairy – Blue Storybooks (Set 6)
Use the 'sad' words from the Power Words Walls, *thinking out loud* other words that mean the same as 'despair.' Ask children to TTYP and decide the words they think are the really sad words – not just a bit sad!
Think of scenarios to use the word
Ask children for fairy stories they know where a character despaired. TTYP and feed back using 'Popcorn': Cinderella, Sleeping Beauty, The Emperor (who had no clothes), The Ugly Duckling... Choose one idea to develop. Ask the children why the character had been in despair e.g. Cinderella.

Either deconstruct a sentence you have prepared earlier (or use the one from the Get Writing! book) showing how you built a mind picture or build the sentence from a simple sentence or sentence stem.

Deconstruct a 'ready-built' sentence
Cinderella sat in ***despair****, hunched in the corner by the fire, weeping, because she could not go to the ball.*

Ask: 'Which words show you the despair Cinderella was feeling? How many words/ phrases?'
TTYP and feed back.
Act out the sentence.
'Are there any other words we could add or change to make a stronger picture of her despair?' For example, describe the corner/ how she was weeping.
Ask the children to think of another time in the story when Cinderella was in despair. See if they can use some of the words in another situation.
Get the children to practise saying their sentence out loud to their partners, before they write.

Build a sentence – starting with a simple sentence
Ask the children to make your sentence into a showing sentence.
Feed in second layer vocabulary and ideas to the children.
Cinderella was in ***despair****.*
Ask: 'Where was Cinderella sitting?' TTYP and feed back.
Rewrite the sentence using one or two of the children's ideas.
Cinderella sat on the cold bare floor in ***despair****.*

Ask: 'How was she sitting?' TTYP and feed back.
Rewrite the sentence using one or two of their ideas.
Cinderella slumped on the cold bare floor in ***despair****.*

Ask: 'Why was she in despair?' TTYP and feed back.
Cinderella slumped on the cold bare floor in ***despair*** *because her sisters had not taken her to the ball.*
Cross out and change words as you go – don't just accept their first ideas.

Build a sentence – starting with a sentence stem
Using a stem:

- start with an adverb: *Despairingly, Cinderella reached for... longingly, Cinderella looked at...*
- start with a verb: *Slumped, in despair, on the cold bare floor... Weeping with despair...*

Model how you take a sentence and play around with the words.
Practise saying the sentences out loud, getting the children to mime the punctuation and discussing how changing the emphasis on different words alters the meaning of the sentence.
Slumped on the cold bare floor, Cinderella wept in despair because her sisters had not taken her to the ball.
Weeping with despair, Cinderella slumped on the cold bare floor, wishing she were at the ball.

Assessment
You will only know if the activity has been successful when children use the vocabulary in their writing at another time.

Key teaching point
Feed in ideas and second layer words - they need this to grow their writing vocabulary.

Activity 7: Edit a sentence

Preparation
Write the sentence on the board - as it is in the Get Writing! book or make your own errors in the sentence.

Purpose
- For children to develop their own editing skills

Teaching time
Partner work: ask partners to read the sentence and tell each other the errors.
Feedback: select children to tell you the errors and correct the errors on your board.
Individual work: ask the children to correct the errors in their Get Writing! books.

Assessment
This activity is used to support children's writing in writing activity 8 and 9.

Key teaching point
- Give a lot of support to children at the earlier stage.
- Adapt the edit to the needs of your group, if necessary. If it is too hard, work out the errors, together as a group, first.
- Make strong links for the children between these editing activities and children editing their own work.

Activities 8 and 9: Picture Strip and Guided Writing

Writing compositions is hard for most children. Coming up with 'imaginative' ideas isn't easy - but remembering the idea while spelling, forming letters (neatly on the line), popping in punctuation; choosing power words, great connectives, gripping openers, and interesting clauses must feel pretty impossible. Never mind the audience, the purpose, the genre (with all its features), and what's more, your partner has taken the best pencil on the table!
Maybe that's why some children spend writing lessons going to the toilet, looking for a pencil/ book/ chair, sharpening a pencil, writing the date, copying the title and the learning objective or just sitting. However excited and creative we are about the task - so many inspiring ideas, so many great props, children don't always feel the same.

The aim in these lessons is to help children to write in bite-sized chunks – using exactly the same techniques as we use for 'build a sentence' to make it easy and fun – to assist them all the way, so they succeed.

The easier they find writing, the more they will choose to write and the greater their success.

These lessons give you a strong structure to build upon. However, as each group of children responds differently and you have your own ideas, the tasks are open enough to have lots of fun with. The success of children's writing depends upon the help you give them. The more you help, the more they will give back.

Preparation

Decide which of the writing activities you will focus upon for this story – or you may decide to do both.

The picture strip is developed with pictures, support sentences, picture bubbles and lots of talk.

The guided writing frames are developed with guide questions and statements, and with support sentences, picture bubbles and plenty of discussion.

You will need to plan the picture strip and the guided writing *before* you start the reading activities, so you can make the most of the opportunities to develop the vocabulary and ideas through the week; by the time your children write they will already have many ideas from your teaching. You will have:

- introduced vocabulary in the 'Vocabulary check', 'Reading with fluency and expression' and 'Build a sentence';
- developed ideas during the 'Introduction' and 'Questions to talk about'
- taught punctuation during 'Reading with fluency and expression' and discussed characters' thoughts, feelings and actions.

Purpose

- For children to write a composition using the pictures/ frames and bubbles and to apply the vocabulary, sentence structures and ideas developed through the week.

Before the children write

- Ensure that you have developed their ideas so they all have something to say.
- After partner discussion, feedback and modelling for each picture or frame, rub out the sentence you have written on the board – though keep up vocabulary words. Encourage the children to write a different sentence – though don't worry if they use the same one.
- When children are at their tables, pencils in hand, ask them to practise saying their own sentence to their partners.
- Encourage them to re-read the sentences to themselves as they write.

While the children are writing

- Walk round all the time – supporting children with ideas and vocabulary – don't leave them to get on with it! Praise children for using specific adventurous vocabulary and ideas.
- Read out sentences – embellish a sentence to encourage children to do the same.
- Help early finishers extend their sentence further or write another sentence.
- Some children will write more than others – due to speed of writing and quickness of thought! Encourage the slower writers – they will only get quicker with practice and praise.

Assessment

Use reading activity 7: 'Edit a sentence'

You will have encouraged children to spell words using current grapheme knowledge so that they choose adventurous vocabulary rather than just the words they can spell correctly.

Tell the children the picture or frame you want them to edit.

Partner work

Ask Partner 1 to help Partner 2 to:

1. tick the 'power' words/phrases – and explain why they have chosen them.
2. in green, draw in the punctuation – add it in if it is not there. Tell them the punctuation you want them to add.
3. in pencil, correct any common spelling errors. Do not use dictionaries to check.

Your marking

Draw wiggly lines under your favourite power words and phrases – with ticks above. Write your comments in response to their ideas and vocabulary.

- In pencil – draw a line under five common words that are misspelled, probably because children's focus was upon their ideas.
- Do not write any negative comments in their books; you have ensured that the children have worked really hard during the lesson.

If you have concerns about their handwriting, address this in your handwriting lessons.

Writing we have edited ourselves...

Display photocopies of the work – with all the editing. Children will see that you value their ideas, even without perfect presentation.

Key teaching points

- Teach creative writing – do not focus on secretarial skills.
- Do not use the picture strip as a dull retell, or allow the children to complete the frame without any support.
- Discuss and then get children to write picture-by-picture, frame-by-frame – don't discuss all of them all at once.
- Don't nag children about their spelling and handwriting while they are focusing on composition.
- Finally – try the writing task yourself before teaching. It will show you how hard writing is and also help you to teach more vocabulary, sentence structures and punctuation effectively.

Teaching time

Example picture strip: Hairy Fairy (from Get Writing! Blue book 6)

Picture 1

Build a sentence-stem with 'thinking' and 'feeling' bubbles
Think out loud how you use the 'feeling bubble'. Give children the possible options for how a character is feeling, e.g. 'Is the fairy feeling excited aboout his new job, or is he feeling apprehensive?' TTYP and feed back using Choral response. Model using the more popular response, e.g. "So you think the fairy was excited about being a fairy but felt that nobody would believe he could be one as he is so hairy. He's flying through the air on his way to his new job. I wonder what he's thinking?'
TTYP. Feed back using 'Choose two'.
Think out loud as you develop one of their ideas, orally, into a longer sentence (example below in italics) e.g. 'I'm going to try so hard to be a brilliant in my new job, *thought the fairy excitedly as he flew to his new job'* or 'I am going to make the fairy queen very proud, *thought the fairy excitedly as he flew to his new job.'*
Mime the punctuation actions as the children repeat each other's sentences – with your additions.

It is not essential to write about every picture. In this example Picture 2 is omitted.

Picture 3

Build a sentence-stem with a 'saying' bubble
Think out loud: 'Mrs Blair moaned a lot about the fairy. She felt very cross and frustrated that she had been sent such an ugly fairy. We were all very good at being Mrs Blair yesterday.'
Partner discussion and feedback
'What did Mrs Blair say? How did she say this?'
Provide the children with a starter and repeat the children's suggestion along with your starter, e.g. *'Mrs Blair stamped her foot in anger,* "Why would anyone think I would want such a horrid ugly fairy. It will have to go!" she grumbled.'

Picture 4

Build a sentence – simple sentence and a 'feeling' bubble
Partner discussion and feedback
Display a simple sentence, e.g. *The fairy sat in the chair all day.*
Think out loud as you take on the role of a particular character. Show how the characters may be saying one thing but thinking something else.
Ask the questions and write children's suggestions on the board. Add your own vocabulary and ideas too.
'What did the fairy feel?' Bored, fed-up, depressed, in despair
'How did the fairy sit in the chair to show he's feeling in depressed?' Slumped, flopped, hunched.
'What did his face look like?' Frowning, mouth turned down
'What did he do in the chair?' Swung his legs, fidgeted, looked out of the window

Explain that now you have a lot of ideas, you will choose one or two to develop a few sentences. Rewrite the sentence using some of the children's ideas. *Think out loud* as you write. Show them how you use insertion marks to add words and cross out words you don't need.
Staring out of the window, the fairy sat in the chair all day.
Staring glumly out of the window, the fairy slumped in the chair all day.
Staring glumly out of the window, watching other fairies go by, the fairy slumped in the hairdresser's black leather chair all day.

Picture 5

Build a sentence-stem with the 'happening' bubble
Think out loud what could be going to happen next, or give further explanation for what is going on.
'Let's remind ourselves of our ideas yesterday. We thought about what Father Christmas would do next.'
Ask children to TTYP, to try putting their own new ending to the story.
Give the children the stem you want them to start with:
After wrapping his last present of the year…
Ask the children to compose sentences with their partners.

Note: Make little bubble icons as cards for the children to keep in their book bags so parents can use them at home when reading stories to the children.

Guided Writing example: Surprise (from Hairy Fairy, Get Writing! Blue book 6)
Introduce the activity
Explain that all night you have been dreaming about flying – flying with large, delicate wings. Shockingly, when you woke up you found it was not a dream. This morning, you woke up with wings…

1. Writing frame: *Describe what you saw when you woke up*
(Build a sentence – start with a stem)
I woke up in the middle of a dream. I felt something...
Ask the children what the wings feel like. Slippery, delicate, smooth
I woke up in the middle of a dream. I felt something delicate and smooth on my back.
What did they look like? Beautiful, transparent, shiny, diaphanous (add this one!), shimmering
Then, I looked in the mirror and saw beautiful shimmering wings on my back.

2. Writing frame: *Describe how you felt*
(Build a sentence – start with simple sentence)
I was worried.
Did you feel anything else? Nervous, like I was going to be sick.
I was so worried that I felt I might be sick.
Why did you feel like this? Friends/ family laugh, have them forever?
I was so worried that I felt I might be sick. Will I have wings forever?

3. Writing frame: *What did you do?*
(Build a sentence – simple sentence)
Tried to cover them up/ Dashed around the room/ Hid under the covers/ Ran into my brother's room to show him
I dashed around the room.
How did you dash? Frantically/ madly/ quickly
Frantically, I dashed around my room.
What did you do? Looked for a coat/ got dressed/ nothing
Frantically, I dashed round my room, looking for my coat
Why did you look for a coat? To hide my wings/ uniform won't fit
Frantically, I dashed round my room, looking for my coat to hide the wings.

4. Writing frame: *What happened when you went into breakfast? What did your family do?*
(Build a sentence – start with a stem)
Cautiously, I crept downstairs and nipped quickly into the kitchen...
What did you see when you went in the kitchen?
Mum eating breakfast/ Dad stacking the dishwasher
Cautiously, I crept downstairs and nipped quickly into the kitchen... Mum was eating her cereal at the kitchen table and Dad had his back to me.
What did they say to you? Hurry up/ Why have you got your coat on? Sit down and have your breakfast
Cautiously, I crept downstairs and nipped quickly into the kitchen...
Mum was eating her cereal at the kitchen table and Dad had his back to me. Mum said 'Hurry up, you'll be late, eat your breakfast.'
And so on...

14 Handwriting

Organise a five-minute daily discrete handwriting lesson with the whole class. This should be at a different time of the day to the phonic lessons.

Use the handwriting picture phrases on the Speed Sounds cards in the Speed Sounds Lessons to practise the formation of letters (for example around the dinosaur's body, up his neck and down to his feet).

Handwriting lessons allow children to put all their energies into the physical process of writing. The children (often boys) who are more likely to avoid choosing play activities involving writing benefit hugely from a focused time when the teacher ensures their handwriting skills develop. And as their skills improve they are more likely to choose these play activities and therefore improve further.

Start to teach a joined script when children can encode quickly and easily using Set 1 and 2 sounds. Teaching joins before this hinders children's speed of encoding. It is vital that children understand that being a good writer is not the same as being a good handwriter.

Help children get into good writing habits. Show them the perfect handwriting position: feet on the floor, chair pulled up - not too close to the table - bottom on seat, one hand holding the paper.

What is the purpose of one-to-one tutoring?

One-to-one tutoring catches children *before* they fall so *all* children learn to read the first time they are taught. It prevents the need for any later intervention.

Why is one-to-one tutoring needed?

Although children are placed into homogeneous groups in *Read Write Inc.* the 'lowest' attaining group have the widest variety of needs and are therefore the least homogeneous group of all.

In order that these children can receive the same carefully targeted RWI teaching as all the other groups of children, some may need one-to-one tutoring for 10 to 20 minutes a day – on top of their group session in the morning.

However, before deciding upon tutoring, the RWI manager needs to be sure that teachers and TAs, taking the lowest progress groups, are teaching RWI to the highest standard; extra support given to the teacher quickly can often result in fewer children needing one-to-one tutoring.

What are children taught during one-to-one tutoring sessions?

Children practise the same Speed Sounds and read the same Ditty/Storybook that they have been taught during the morning RWI group session.

When should one-to-one tutoring be introduced?

One-to-one tutoring should be introduced as soon as a child cannot make good progress in the 'lowest' attaining group. Children making progress in this group may not need tutoring. Vulnerable children in Reception should receive tutoring as soon as they start the programme.

Which children should receive one-to-one tutoring?

Children who need tutoring come from two broad groups:

1 *Children who cannot read but do **not** have any recognised special need*

This group may include children in Years R to 6 (P1–7) who:

- have missed schooling or changed schools
- are newly arrived to Britain - and are at an early stage of learning English
- have very poor concentration
- have fluctuating hearing loss (glue ear) – and may find it difficult to flourish in a larger group.

It may also contain children who are considered to be dyslexic and older children who, in the first year of introducing RWI, are significantly behind their peers. These are the children who have suffered the most from the lack of quality first teaching using a systematic, structured phonics programme (ABT: Ain't Been Taught children).

All these children will be able to access the rest of the curriculum as soon as they can read effectively.

2 *Children who cannot read and do have a recognised special need*

This group consists of SEN children with more complex needs who will need long term support. These children will have significant and particular needs that will continue throughout life, e.g. children who are on the autistic spectrum and those with global delay. Many of these children would previously have been educated in a special school.

How many weeks should children be tutored for?

Children who cannot read but do not have a recognised special need

The period given is approximate – the time given is as much dependent on the quality of the teaching as the child's ability to learn.

Note: not all children need to be tutored at all reading stages, if they can achieve the target without tutoring.

As each RWI year progresses, fewer and fewer children will need tutoring.
One-to-one tutoring lists: 10-20 minutes a day.
There are five targets. Decide which of the five targets the children should start with.

Target A learn Set 1 Speed Sounds: two to six weeks

Target B learn sound-blending: one to four weeks

Target C practise reading the Ditties: four to eight weeks

Target D learn Set 2 Speed Sounds: two to four weeks

Target E practise reading the Green, Purple, Pink and Orange Storybooks: four to eight weeks (or longer if the school can accommodate this)

Some schools continue to provide tutoring for their most vulnerable children until they are fluent readers.
Children must not be moved on to the next target until they have achieved the previous one.

Children who cannot read and have a recognised special need
These children may need *significant* tutoring depending upon the severity of their need.

How many children should be tutored?

The number of children needing one-to-one tutoring is dependent upon four key factors:

- The quality of the teaching in the morning RWI sessions – get this right and the numbers for tutoring will fall dramatically.
- The length of time the school has implemented RWI – after two years of implementation very few older children need tutoring.
- The level of mobility – some schools have a steady influx of new children in all age groups unable to read.
- The number of children with definite special needs – these children may need tutoring for much longer.

What percentage of children will need tutoring?

The number of 'ABT' children tutored will reduce year by year. In a school with low mobility, the percentage will drop from about 10% in the first year to 5% in the second year to 1-2% in subsequent years.

Will any children fail to read?

We do not expect any children to fail to read; although in rare cases some children who have severe cognition and learning disability and who are functioning at a very early developmental stage may progress very slowly.

Who should be trained as reading tutors?

The RWI manager and between two and five tutors are trained depending upon the size of the school and the mobility of children.
Individual special needs assistants should also be trained to work with SEN children.
Headteachers are encouraged to select teaching assistants and special needs assistants from their *existing staff* who have a total commitment and a genuine passion for teaching children to read.
It is particularly effective when senior teachers without class responsibility, including the headteacher, tutor at least one child. This sends a strong message to staff and parents – this school is serious about getting every child to read.

These tutors will become 'real' experts in the skills of teaching reading to challenging children therefore benefiting *all* the children they work with throughout the day.

Who will manage the tutoring programme?

The in-school RWI manager will work with the trained tutors to plan the tutoring for each child based on a comprehensive assessment of their starting point, and analysis of their specific need.

How long will the training be?

The tutors and the RWI manager will already have received the basic two-day RWI Phonic training. The manager and tutors, together, practise the teaching activities in the One-to-one tutoring guide, on pages 95–99, using the RWI Training DVD to support.

About three twilight sessions or one full day (run by the RWI manager) is needed at the start. Then, plan review sessions to discuss progress of the children and share best practice every four weeks. If however RWI managers would like further support in order to do this, courses are run by Ruth Miskin Literacy, see www.ruthmiskinliteracy.com.

How is consistency maintained?

Progress checks should be made by the RWI manager to monitor the rate of progress and to ensure the quality of teaching in both the morning group sessions and afternoon tutoring slots.

One-to-one tutoring guide

Target A To read Set 1 Speed Sounds quickly and easily

Share the target with the child.

Choose four sound cards that the child cannot read easily - it does not matter in which order they are taught. Aim to get four new cards a day into the child's Speed Sound pack of sounds that they know.

Always praise – a lot!

Step 1

- Teach the four sounds using the *Speed Sounds Lesson Plans*: say the sound, read the sound, write only briefly. Do this as quickly as possible – he may only need reminding.
- Check he understands that the picture is the same shape as the letter.
- Run you finger round the snake - sssssssssssnake. Run your finger round the s and say ssssssss. Same, same!

Now follow the next steps. These are very small, so some children will not need to go through them all.

Step 2

- Show the four cards, *picture* side up, e.g. snake mountain apple dinosaur.
- Ask the child to *point* as you say the picture *words*: snake mountain apple dinosaur.
- Then, ask the child to *say* the picture card *words* in and out of order – as you point.
- Repeat until speedy.

Step 3

- Show the same cards - picture side up again.
- Ask the child to *point* to the card as you stretch / bounce the sound before you say the name of the picture e.g. sssssssssssnake (stretch), d-d-d-dinosaur (bounce) mmmmmmountain, a-a-a-a-apple.
  Make this into a game. See if he can point to the card while you are still stretching or bouncing – before you say the actual word.

- Ask the child to *say* the sound, stretching or bouncing as you point.
  (Only get the child to do this when he is good at pointing.)
- Repeat until speedy.

Step 4

Show the same cards, again, *picture* side up.

- Ask the child to choose a card he would like to turn over to the letter side.
- Ask him to say the sound without the help of the picture. If he forgets the sound turn the card back to the picture side.

Get the child to say, for example, 'the snake looks like the sss'.
Repeat turning the cards from the pictures to the letters until he can say all four sounds in response to just the letter sound.

Step 5

Now show the cards *letter* side up.

- Ask the child to *point* to the card as you say the short sound, e.g. 's'.
- Ask the child to *say* the short sound as you point.
- Repeat until speedy.

Repeat Steps 1–5 until the child has built a pack of Set 1 cards that he can read at speed. These are the cards that children will practise blending into words.

Target B **To sound-blend three- and four-sound words using Set 1 Speed Sounds**

Share the target with the child.
Once the child can read most of the Set 1 sounds, start sound blending, but continue to practise reading all the Speed Sounds Set 1 cards as a warm-up.

N.B. Only blend with sounds the child can read very quickly and easily.
Follow the assisted blending (Steps 1–3 below), until you know the child is ready to blend independently.
Select three cards, that the child can read at speed, to make a word (include a, e, i, or u).

Assisted blending
Example word: mat

Step 1

First orally, without the cards:

1. Ask the child to look at your mouth as you say the sounds in an exaggerated manner: 'm – a – t'. Really feel those sounds!
   Repeat a few times.
2. Ask the child to look at your mouth as you say the whole word 'mat' in an exaggerated manner: mat

Step 2

Blending - *with* the cards
Model how you:

1. Say 'mat' clearly again.
   Say: I will need: 'm', 'a' and 't' – as you place the sound cards on the table
2. Point to the sound cards as you say 'm - a - t'.
3. Sweep your finger under the word and say 'mat' – in an exaggerated manner
   Take away the cards and repeat 1 and 2.
   Really feel the sounds as you say the whole word!
   Get the child to copy.

Step 3

1. Ask the child to close his eyes while you muddle the three sound cards.
2. Give the child the cards to make the words again.
3. Ask him to point to the cards as he says the sounds and then the word. Repeat.

Independent blending

When the child can make the words quickly in 'assisted blending', help him blend independently. If this is a step too far, continue 'assisted blending'.

- Put out m, a, t sound cards onto the table – silently.
- Ask the children to say and point to the sounds and then read the word.

Repeat a few times.

Repeat until he can read nonsense words with three and four Set 1 sound cards.

Praise – a lot!

Target C To read the Ditty texts independently

Share the target with the child.

Practise the Ditty he will read with his reading group the next day.

Step 1

Ask the child to read Set 1 cards at speed. Review any sounds that he needs to practise. Check that he knows the sounds he will need to read the Ditty – particularly sounds with double letters ll, ss, ck, ng, nk, ch, sh, th.

Step 2

Write the Ditty words on cards or paper before the lesson.

Ask the child to read the words in Fred Talk and then say the word.

If he has difficulty, show him how you exaggerate the pronunciation of the sounds and then the word.

Practise until the child can sound out the words very quickly.

Step 3

Ask the child to read the Ditty a few times until he can read it without Fred Talk.

Talk about the Ditty together.

Continue to practise reading the Ditties until he can read the later Ditties with very little support.

Target D To read Set 2 Speed Sounds at speed – on cards and in words

Share the target with the child.

Choose three sound cards that he cannot read easily - it does not matter in which order they are taught.

Aim to get two or three new cards a day into the child's Speed Sound pack. Include Set 1 and 2 sounds, as they are taught. *Do not use letter names at any point.*

Decide the best step to start – some children will not need to go through all the steps with every sound.

Step 1

Example: ay ee igh

- Show the three cards, *picture* side up:
  ay: May I play?
  ee: What can you see?
  igh: Fly high.
- Ask the child to **point** as you say the picture *phrases.*
- Then, ask the child to **say** the *phrase* in and out of order at speed.
- Repeat until speedy.

Step 2

- Show the same cards – *picture* side up again.
- Ask the child to **point** to the card as you say *just* the sound: ee, ay, igh – in and out of order.
- Ask the child to **say** the sound as you point. (Only get the child to do this when he is good at pointing.)
- Repeat until speedy.

Step 3

Show the same cards, again, *picture* side up.

- Ask the child to choose a card he would like to turn over to the letter side.
- Ask him to say the sound without the help of the picture. If he forgets, turn the card back to the picture side.

Get the child to say, for example, '"May I play?" helps me remember the sound ay.'
Repeat turning the cards from the pictures to the letters until he can say all three sounds in response to just the letter.

Step 4

Now show the cards *letter* side up.

- Ask the child to **point** to the card and as you say the sound.
- Ask the child to **say** the short sound as you point.
- Repeat until speedy.

Step 5

Mix up the Green Word cards containing the sounds you have just practised e.g. ay, ee, and igh, mixed in with a few Green Word cards from Set 1.
Ask the child to read each word in Fred Talk and then say the word.
Repeat Steps 1-5 until the child has built a pack of Set 2 cards that he can:

- read at speed when mixed up with Set 1 Speed Sound cards.
- read at speed in a mixed set of Green Word cards.

Praise – a lot!

Target E **To read the Green and Purple Storybooks independently**

Share the target with the child.
Once most of the children have achieved targets A–E provide one-to-one tutoring for children who are making the slowest progress in the Storybook groups. Keep going until every child can read the Grey level books.

Step 1

Ask the child to read Set 1 and 2 Speed Sounds. Review any sounds that he needs to practise. Check that he can read the sounds he will need to read the Storybook – particularly sounds with double letters ll, ss, ck, ng, nk, ch, sh, th and any from Speed Sounds Set 2.

Step 2

Ask the child to read the Green Words (listed in the book) in Fred Talk and then say the word.
If he has difficulty, exaggerate the pronunciation of the sounds and the word.
Keep practising until the child can say the words without saying the sounds first – if possible.
Ask him to read the Red Words.

Step 3

Ask the child to read the story a few times until he can read it without Fred Talk.
Talk about the story together after each page.
Praise – a lot!

Curriculum reading levels

England: Approximate NC level for reading if decoding well and understanding texts	England: P Scales	Scotland: 5-14 Programme level	Scotland: Curriculum for Excellence	Wales: National Curriculum	Northern Ireland: Northern Ireland Curriculum	Storybooks completed	Speed Sounds known effortlessly and blending
	P6	A	Early	Outcome 2			Set 1
	P7/P8	A	Early	Outcome 3		Ditties	Set 1
1c		A	Early	Level 1	Level 1	Green	Set 1
1c		A	Early	Level 1	Level 1	Purple	Set 1
1c/1b		A	Early	Level 1	Level 1	Pink	Sets 1 + 2
1b/1a		A	Early	Level 1	Level 1	Orange	Sets 1 + 2
1a/2c		A	Early	Level 1/2	Level 1/2	Yellow	Sets 1, 2 + 3 (ea, a-e, i-e, o-e, u-e)
2b		A	Early	Level 2	Level 2	Blue	Sets 1, 2 + 3
2a+		B	First	Level 2	Level 2	Grey	Sets 1, 2 + 3
3		B	First	Level 3	Level 3	*Read Write Inc. Comprehension*	Sets 1, 2 + 3

Letters and Sounds and *Read Write Inc. Phonics* correlation chart

<table>
<tr><th colspan="3">Progression in Letters and Sounds</th><th>Read Write Inc. Phonics</th></tr>
<tr><td rowspan="5">Phase 1 continuous through Phase 2-6 Show awareness of rhyme and alliteration. Distinguish between different sounds in the environment and phonemes. Explore and experiment with sounds and words.</td><td colspan="2">Phase 2
Working on: Using common consonants and vowels. Blending for reading and segmenting for spelling simple CVC words.
Working on: Knowing that words are constructed from phonemes and that phonemes are represented by graphemes.
Letter progression:
Set 5: h, b, f, ff, l, ll, ss
Set 4: ck, e, u, r,
Set 3: g. o. c. k
Set 2: i, n, m, d
Set 1: s, a, t, p</td><td>Speed Sounds Set 1, Ditties, Green and Purple books</td></tr>
<tr><td>Phase 3 (YR/P1)
Working on: Knowing one grapheme for each of the phonemes</td><td>Working on: Reading and spelling a wide range of CVC words using all letters and less frequent consonant digraphs and some long vowel phonemes.
Graphemes:
ear, air, ure, er,
ar, or, ur, ow, oi,
ai, ee, igh, oa, oo
Working on: Reading and spelling CVC words using a wider range of letters, short vowels, some consonant digraphs and double letters.
Consonant digraphs:
ch, sh, th, ng
Working on: Reading and spelling CVC words using letters and short vowels.
Letter progression
Set 7: y, z, zz, qu
Set 6: j, v, w, x</td><td>Speed Sounds Set 2, Pink and Orange books</td></tr>
<tr><td colspan="2">Phase 4 (YR-Y1/P1-P2)
Working on: Segmenting adjacent consonants in words and apply this in spelling.
Working on: Blending adjacent consonants in words and applying this skill when reading unfamiliar texts.</td><td>Revision of Speed Sounds Set 2, Pink, Orange and Yellow books</td></tr>
<tr><td colspan="2">Phase 5 (Y1/P2)
Working on: Reading phonically decodable two-syllable and three-syllable words.
Working on: Using alternative ways of pronouncing and spelling the graphemes corresponding to the long vowel phonemes.
Working on: Spelling complex words using phonically plausible attempts.</td><td>Speed Sounds Set 3, Blue books</td></tr>
<tr><td colspan="2">Phase 6 (Y2/P3)
Working on: Recognising phonic irregularities and becoming more secure with less common grapheme-phoneme correspondences
Working on: Applying phonic skills and knowledge to recognize and spell an increasing number of complex words.</td><td>Revision of Speed Sounds Set 3 and Grey books</td></tr>
</table>

Speed Sounds used in the Storybooks

Children should know the Speed Sounds listed before reading each book

Ditty Photocopy Masters	Set 1	Ditty books	Set 1

Green Set 1 Storybooks (70-100 words)

On the bus	Set 1	Tug, tug	Set 1
My dog Ned	Set 1	Chips	Set 1
Six fish	Set 1	The web	Set 1
The spell	Set 1	Pip's pizza	Set 1
Black Hat Bob	Set 1	Stitch the witch	Set 1

Purple Set 2 Storybooks (70-100 words)

Ken's cap	Set 1	Elvis	Set 1
A bad fox	Set 1	Flip Frog and the bug	Set 1
Big Blob and Baby Blob	Set 1	Red Ken	Set 1
Tim and Tom	Set 1	Billy the Kid	Set 1
Tag	Set 1	In the bath	Set 1

Pink Set 3 Storybooks (150 words)

Scruffy Ted	Set 1	Sanjay stays in bed	Sets 1, 2: ay
Tab the cat	Set 1	The greedy green gremlin	+ ee
In the sun	Set 1	In the night	+ igh
The dressing up box	Set 1	Snow	+ ow
Tab's kitten	Set 1	So cool	+ oo

Orange Set 4 Storybooks (150 words)

Playday	Sets 1, 2: ay	Come on Margo!	+ ar
I think I want to be a bee	+ ee	My sort of horse	+ or
A bad fright	+ igh	Haircuts	+ air
Follow me!	+ ow	My best shirt	+ ir
Too much!	+ oo	Look out!	+ ou
A good cook?	+ *oo*	Hunt the tortoise	+ oy

Yellow Set 5 Storybooks (250 words)

The duckchick	Set 1	Lost	+ ay
Off sick	Set 1	Do we have to keep it?	+ ee
Tom Thumb	Set 1	Danny and the bump-a-lump	+ igh
The gingerbread man	Set 1	Grow your own radishes	+ ow
Robin Hood	Sets 1, 2: *oo*	The foolish witch	+ oo

Blue Set 6 Storybooks (300 words)

Barker	Sets 1, 2: ay ee igh ow oo *oo* ar	The jar of oil	Set 1 + oy oi
That poor goose	+ or	Jade's party	Sets 1, 2, 3: a-e
Hairy fairy	+ air	Jellybean	+ ea
King of the birds	+ ir	A box full of light	+ i-e
Our house	+ ou	A hole in the hill	+ o-e

Grey Set 7 Storybooks (350 words)

Rex to the rescue	Sets 1, 2, 3: a-e + ea + i-e + o-e u-e	Toad	+ oa
		Andrew	+ ew
The lion's paw	+ aw	Dear Vampire	+ ire
I dare you	+ are	Vulture Culture	+ ure
Looking after a hamster	+ er	A celebration on planet Zox	+ tion
How silly	+ ow (as in cow)	Dangerous Dinosaur	+ tious cious
Wailing Winnie's car boot sale	+ ai	The invisible clothes	+ ible able

Further practice of the sounds is provided by the Non-fiction books and the Set A Storybooks.

Red Words used in the Ditties and Storybooks

Display the Red Words on a Red Word Wall as soon as it has been introduced in the Ditty or Storybook. These words contain graphemes that are not on the chart representing the sound in these words. The grey letters show you the 'grotty' grapheme, that is not listed on the grapheme chart.

I the you your said was are of want what they

to do does all call tall small any many anyone

some come watch who where there here were

brother other mother father love above two once buy

worse walk talk caught bought thought through

wear whole could would should great son water

Red 'for a while' Words

These include graphemes that have not been taught by the time they are needed in the reading books. As soon as the grapheme has been taught, each of these turn into a Green Word!

he me we she be no so go old her saw my

by why now how down over school

Simple Speed Sounds chart

Consonants: *stretchy*

f	l	m	n	r	s	v	z	sh	th	ng nk

Consonants: *bouncy*

b	c k	d	g	h	j	p	qu	t	w	x	y	ch

Vowels: *bouncy*

a	e	i	o	u

Vowels: *stretchy*

ay	ee	igh	ow

Vowels: *stretchy*

oo	oo	ar	or	air	ir	ou	oy

Complex Speed Sounds chart

Consonants: *stretchy*

f	l	m	n	r	s	v	z	sh	th	ng
ff	ll	mm	nn	rr	ss	ve	zz	ti		nk
ph	le	mb	kn	wr	se		s	ci		
					c					
					ce					

Consonants: *bouncy*

b	c	d	g	h	j	p	qu	t	w	x	y	ch
bb	k	dd	gg		g	pp		tt	wh			tch
	ck				ge							
	ch											

Vowels

a	e	i	o	u	ay	ee	igh	ow
	ea				a-e	y	i-e	o-e
					ai	ea	ie	oa
						e	i	o

oo	oo	ar	or	air	ir	ou	oy	ire	ear	ure
u-e			oor	are	ur	ow	oi			
ue			ore		er					
ew			aw							
			au							

Speed Sounds

This chart shows the three sets of Speed Sounds for children to learn.

Speed Sounds	
Simple Speed Sounds chart **one sound – one grapheme**	**Complex Speed Sounds chart** **one sound – many graphemes**
Speed Sounds Set 1: m a s d t i n p g o c k u b f e l h sh r j v y w th z ch q x ng nk **Speed Sounds Set 2:** ay ee igh ow oo oo ar or air ir ou oy	**Speed Sounds Sets 1 and 2 and** **Speed Sounds Set 3:** a-e ea i-e o-e u-e aw are ur er ow ai oa ew ire ear ure tious tion

Glossary of terms

Fred Talk: Fred is a puppet who says, reads and spells words in pure sounds; he never says the whole word so the children do this for him
He never adds 'uh' after a consonant sound e.g. fuh luh muh
(A slight 'uh' cannot be helped when saying the sounds b, d, g, j, w, and y)

Grapheme: One letter or one group of letters used to write one sound e.g.
The sound 'f' can be written with the grapheme **f** (**f**un), **ff** (hu**ff**)
The sound 'igh' can be written with the grapheme **igh** (n**igh**t) or **i** (kn**i**fe) or **ie** (t**ie**)

Green words: Words made up of graphemes that children have been taught. Children use 'Fred Talk' to read and 'Fred Fingers' to spell these words

Red words: Common words with an uncommon spelling e.g. said, would, bought

Challenge words: Topical words particular to a story

Syllables: Chunks within long words

Root: The part of the word that gives the most meaning